COOL KITCHEN

COOL
KITCHEN

No Oven, No Stove, No Sweat!

125 Delicious, No-Work Recipes for
Summertime or Anytime

LAUREN CHATTMAN

William Morrow and Company, Inc.
New York

For Jack and Rose

Library of Congress Cataloging-in-Publication Data
Chattman, Lauren.
　Cool kitchen : No oven, no stove, no sweat!
125 delicious, no-work recipes for summertime or anytime / Lauren Chattman.—1st ed.
　　p.　cm
　Includes index.
　ISBN 0-688-15513-8
　1. Cookery.　I. Title.
TX714.C4662　1998
641.5′64—dc21
97-25661
CIP

Printed in the United States of America

First Edition

1　2　3　4　5　6　7　8　9　10

BOOK DESIGN BY MARYSARAH QUINN

www.williammorrow.com

Acknowledgments

My agent, Angela Miller, helped me draft the proposal for this project and turn it into a real book.

Mark Bittman and John Willoughby offered early and much-appreciated support.

I was so thrilled when Pam Hoenig liked the idea of *Cool Kitchen*. Her enthusiasm inspired me during the recipe-developing and testing phase.

It was a pleasure to work with my smart and careful editor, Naomi Glikman.

At home, Yvette Willock provided her invaluable services as taster and baby-sitter.

Special thanks to Jack Bishop for constant encouragement and for eating cool food all winter.

CONTENTS

Introduction

Dreaming of a Cool Kitchen

One 95°F day last summer, steam fogging up my glasses as I overturned a bubbling ten-gallon pot of arborio rice pudding into a plastic container, I moaned to myself, "Would it be so wrong to serve berries and ice cream for dessert?" I was working as a pastry chef at Nick and Toni's, a popular restaurant in the resort community of East Hampton, Long Island. I spent June, July, and August in a non–air-conditioned kitchen turning out individual fruit cobblers, espresso custards, and flourless chocolate cakes by the dozens. It was a great job. But every once in a while, I'll admit, the heat got to me.

As I boiled sugar syrup for my caramel, I'd think up desserts that didn't require 15,000 BTUs—fresh figs with sweetened mascarpone, cherries soaked in kirsch and poured over the richest chocolate sorbet. I'd think about what I wanted for dinner when I got home—nothing hot, just a cool salad with ripe red tomatoes, fresh goat cheese, cubes of bread, and herbs. One day I had a

flash of insight: maybe millions of other hot, tired, hungry people were having these same thoughts. A book idea was born.

Was it brilliance? Or idiocy? I rushed home from work that night to consult with my husband, a cookbook author many times over. "A cookbook of food that's not cooked?" He thought about it for a few seconds as I hovered tensely. Stunned by the simple practicality of the idea, he wondered why nobody had thought of it before.

I got to work, thinking seriously about how I could make great meals without turning on the oven or stove. Once I began, I thought my head would explode with all the ideas I had. What about ten quick, no-cook ways to dress up store-bought rotisserie chicken? Or a whole menu of "cool" appetizers for a quick but elegant cocktail party spread? Wouldn't it be great to have a repertoire of main-course salads that could be fixed in minutes?

I started to think about "cooking" in a brand-new way. The challenge was to prepare food without heat. But once I started coming up with recipes, fixing dinner wasn't a challenge at all. It became fresh, fast, and fun. Just knowing that I would come home from work and be able to sit down to a crab and frisée salad with curry dressing in about ten minutes forced me to give up any thoughts of having a bowl of cereal in front of the television. After a day of peeling fruit and pulling cakes out of the oven, I was excited about getting home from work and cooking again. The food was new. It was delicious. It was cool.

"Hot" Food, Cool Kitchen

I've always looked for ways to enjoy seasonal ingredients and new tastes without heating up the kitchen. My files are stuffed with recipes for cold soups, spicy fruit chutneys, and pestos. Even in the dead of winter I enjoy hearty sandwiches, crisp salads, and simple fruit desserts when I don't have a lot of time but still crave fresh flavors. I know I'm not alone.

Americans now place a premium on fresh ingredients and the time it takes to prepare them. I'm more interested in tasting Thai basil in a quickly mixed dipping sauce than making traditional stocks and stews. Instead of laboring over an elaborate (and

fattening) layer cake to end a family meal, I'd rather sprinkle local peaches with wine and savor some extra time with my dessert. Does this sound familiar? If so, read on.

When I was growing up, my Mom wouldn't have been able to buy daikon radish, fresh papaya, or fish sauce, much less know what to do with them. Now both of us routinely wrap salsa and leftover flank steak in corn tortillas and use soy sauce and wasabi to turn up the volume on a vinaigrette. Quick, fresh, and cosmopolitan, *Cool Kitchen* documents this revolution. My recipes are not slavishly authentic, nor are they forced efforts to combine ingredients in bizarre new ways. When I cook with ethnic ingredients, I try to stay true to the spirit of the dish while adapting it to suit my own tastes and time constraints. Are you interested in incorporating new flavors into your everyday food, but don't have the time to master the art of world cuisines? Me, too.

Even if you've memorized Julia Child, there are times when you just don't feel like digging into (or slaving over) a steaming pot of *boeuf bourguignon*. *Cool Kitchen* is a book for beginners—imagine so many nutritious and interesting dishes that are literally tossed together. But it also contains enough new and innovative ideas about "raw" food to interest and enchant experienced cooks. Fix an instant rice noodle salad for lunch; add an interesting new pesto to a favorite Italian menu; mix some spicy coleslaw while your partner grills a steak; make a chicken sandwich with leftover chicken, some chili-mango chutney, and a baguette; or design and put together an entire warm-weather feast for friends—everything from marinated olives to scallop seviche to water-melon ices—without turning on the stove.

Triumph of Cool Cooking

What started out as a way of eating well while staying cool has turned into something much more. With over one hundred recipes, this book charts a new way of thinking about what and how to cook for dinner. Of course, I haven't thrown out my oven and stove. But now I see that making delicious, interesting, healthy meals doesn't have to involve a lot of cooking. You can broil a piece of fish and fix a spicy Asian coleslaw or a peach and tomato salad to make a special meal. Moreover, you can prepare a salmon fillet ten times and serve it with ten different accompaniments to make it new each time.

Sandwiches, always a convenience food, become surprisingly exciting when spread with chipotle mayonnaise (two minutes in the food processor) or layered with eggplant and peppers from the local Italian deli. I was amazed and delighted at the many no-bake desserts I was able to dream up that turned out to be more fun and satisfying than a Pepperidge Farm cookie or a dish of artificial-tasting extruded frozen yogurt. Fresh berries are always great, but they become extraordinary when gently bathed in sparkling wine. Taste my melon and mango with yogurt "crème fraîche" and you just might put your cake pans into storage.

Recipes for a Cool Kitchen

The recipes that follow are organized into five chapters: Starters and Soups; Salads; Sandwiches; Salsas, Sauces, and Dressings; and Simple Fruit Desserts. One thing that I've learned while writing this book, however, is that categories can be arbitrary and limiting. For example, I created an easy and delicious lemony white bean dip one night for the Starters chapter, but I wound up spreading it on grilled bread and serving it with a green salad for a tasty vegetarian dinner. Wanting to create a simple fruit and cheese dessert, I mixed seedless grapes and French Roquefort. Then I wound up serving it as an appetizer salad. If you're not using the oven or stove, cooking can be improvisational and positively liberating. Use these recipes to try new things and satisfy any crazy cravings and whims.

Cool Kitchen ends with menu suggestions, offering meals made entirely from recipes in the book, as well as ideas on how to supplement the staples in almost everybody's kitchen. Turn to the menu when you invite a few friends over for a weeknight dinner and want to amaze them with a meal of fusilli with Raw Puttanesca Sauce, a green salad, and Strawberries, Red Wine, and Cream. Or just look at the appendix for quick inspiration. When entertaining my Dad, I grill some chicken and serve it with Red Chili Pepper Sauce with Raisins, corn on the cob, and a Bread Salad with Goat Cheese and Navy Beans. This might not be quite the dinner you had in mind for your Dad, but how about serving your brother and sister-in-law a meal of pork tenderloin with Peach Chutney, steamed broccoli, and Minted Chickpea Salad?

Although I started this book in the summer, I've discovered (I'm writing now in the middle of February) that many *Cool Kitchen* concepts work throughout the year. Sun-dried tomato and olive pesto is a great cold weather topping for hot pasta. A Spanish chef's salad with Serrano ham, Manchego cheese, turkey, and roasted peppers makes a scrumptious lunch any time of year. Grapefruit drizzled with Campari is a sunny, invigorating dessert in the dead of winter. If you're like me, you want stylish, flavorful, healthy, and simple food for all seasons. I hope you'll find this food in the pages that follow. ❖

COOL KITCHEN

To prepare meals the *Cool Kitchen* way, it helps to have a pantry stocked with items that add flavor but don't require cooking. It's also helpful to have frozen cooked shrimp on hand and to know how and where to buy cooked chicken. Here's a list of the things I use most often in this book to spice up my favorite no-cook dishes:

Anchovies: Canned or bottled, flat anchovy fillets are instant flavor enhancers. They are a staple of Mediterranean cooking, and even those of you who hate them on top of pizza have undoubtedly enjoyed dishes to which they've been added. Before being used, anchovies should be rinsed under cold water and patted dry to remove excess salt and oil.

Asian Sesame Oil: An oil made from toasted sesame seeds that has a rich flavor and aroma. It is used in dressings as a seasoning and is available in Asian markets and almost all supermarkets.

Capers: The unopened buds of a flowering bush that grows all along the Mediterranean. They are salted and packed in brine. Chopped or used whole, they add a piquant flavor to Mediterranean salads, sandwiches, and dressings. Bottled capers will keep in the refrigerator for two months.

Bottled Roasted Red Peppers, Bottled Artichoke Hearts, Bottled Eggplant, Bottled Hot Peppers: I could devote an entire shelf in my refrigerator to prepared vegetables that have been bottled and imported from Italy. Roasted red bell peppers have countless uses in antipasti, salad dressings, and sandwiches. Marinated artichoke hearts are another favorite. The packager has done all of the work for you—trimming, seasoning, and cooking the vegetables so they are tender and flavorful. Artichokes are great in salads, on sandwiches, and puréed to make dips and spreads. Ditto for bottled eggplant. Pickled hot peppers add instant zing to all kinds of sauces, sandwiches, and spreads. I chop a few and throw them into whatever I'm cooking when I want something spicy and crunchy.

Canned Beans: They are a wonderful help in preparing healthy, tasty no-cook dishes. I purée them for dips; toss them with herbs, lemon juice, and olive oil for quick side dishes; or incorporate them into salads with chicken or seafood. Before using, I drain the beans in a colander and rinse with cold water to wash away any packing liquid and excess salt. I always buy organic brands like Eden or American Prairie. They are not mushy and salty, as many other common brands are.

Canned Tuna: Even people who don't ever cook usually have a can of tuna in the cabinet. It is great on sandwiches and in salads and you can do a lot more with tuna than just mixing it with mayo and chopped celery. Tuna packed in olive oil is rich and delicious, but if you're counting calories, tuna packed in water is fine.

Chilies: I love cold food spiced with chilies. I keep a variety of fresh and dried chilies around so that I can prepare "hot" no-cook dishes on a moment's notice. Most often, I'll turn to my trusty bottle of hot red pepper flakes. A few shakes add instant heat. I also love dried New Mexico chilies that I store in a plastic bag at room temperature and rehydrate with hot water. Just place the chilies in a heat-proof bowl, cover with hot tap water, and let them stand until softened, thirty to forty minutes. They're more complex than hot red pepper flakes. Chipotle chilies in adobo are my new favorite. I buy them in cans at my supermarket (you may have to go to a Latin grocery) and keep them, sauce and all, in an airtight container in the refrigerator for up to a month. Chipotles are hot, but also have a fantastic smoky flavor that's great in all kinds of dips and dressings. I buy jalapeño and red Thai chilies when I want something hot and fresh.

Cooked Chicken: Okay, chicken isn't really a pantry item, but its popularity and easy availability have certainly made it one of the great convenience foods of the nineties. Whole cooked chickens, chicken parts, and boneless breasts are as easy to pick up on the way home as a quart of milk. I'm pretty wary of some of the chicken for sale at delis and take-out shops. Sometimes it is of low quality, flavorless, and rubbery. If you buy cooked chicken, make sure it's the kind of chicken you would cook for yourself if you had time. Look for a place that sells a high-quality brand, like Bell and Evans or Empire. Or try organic or free-range varieties—available at butcher shops and many deluxe supermarkets. These labels do not guarantee freshness, but sometimes mean better flavor and texture than most national, mass-produced brands.

Dried Fruits: Raisins, apricots, figs, dates, and prunes are all packed with flavor. I use dried fruits often in both sweet and savory dishes when I want them to be extra rich and exotic without being high in fat. I keep small quantities of all of these fruits in my pantry. Dried fruit will keep for two or three months if packed in airtight containers or zipper-lock plastic bags.

Fish Sauce: Americans have begun to explore with this Thai product in a big way. Fish sauce, like anchovies, adds a distinctive but not at all fishy flavor to sauces and dressings. Fish sauce is available at Asian groceries and many supermarkets.

 Frozen Shrimp: Unless you live very close to a source for fresh shrimp, chances are that the shrimp you see at your fish market arrived frozen and were then thawed at the market. This is why I prefer shrimp from the freezer case to shrimp that are sold loose from behind the counter. There's a better chance that they will taste fresh when defrosted. Frozen shrimp are available cooked and uncooked. If you buy them cooked, all you need to do is place them in a colander and thaw them out under cold running water for five minutes before using. I keep a couple of twelve-ounce bags of cooked frozen shrimp in my freezer (they'll keep for about one month) so that when the urge strikes I can put together a quick seafood meal in minutes.

Herbs: One of the goals of these recipes is clean, fresh flavor. There is nothing like fresh herbs to lend quality to no-cook dishes. I always have one or two bunches of herbs on hand in the crisper drawer of my refrigerator. I wrap the stem end of the bunch in a damp paper towel and then put the bunch in a zipper-lock plastic bag. Herbs will remain fresh this way for two or three days. I have pretty flexible notions about herbs. If I realize I'm out of parsley when a recipe calls for it, I'll substitute basil. The finished dish will taste different, but the freshness and flavor of the basil will still make it taste great. One thing I rarely do is substitute dried for fresh. You might get good flavor from dried herbs, but you'll never get the color and texture that fresh herbs lend, and that are so important in making appetizing "cool" meals.

Lemons: I always have a few lemons in the refrigerator. I use fresh lemon juice and zest to flavor all kinds of salads, sandwich dressings, and fruit desserts. Look for lemons with smooth skins, no blemishes, and no soft spots. Lemons will keep in the refrigerator for one to two weeks.

Nuts: Nuts add rich texture and flavor to sauces, salads, and desserts. Nuts contain a lot of oil and, if stored at room temperature, may turn rancid. But they will stay fresh for three or four months if packed in zipper-lock plastic bags and frozen.

Olives: Olives are indispensable in cooking and in showing hospitality. I always have black and green marinated olives on hand to offer with a drink to unexpected visitors. I chop them up to put them on salads and in sandwiches. I make olive paste for pasta and pizza. I haven't yet figured out how to work them into dessert, but . . . Seriously,

olives are a great thing. Pick up jars of black kalamata and green Sicilian varieties at the supermarket and keep them in your refrigerator. (We are *not* talking about the canned, pitted California types that have absolutely no flavor.) I'm sure you'll soon be seeking out more exotic varieties such as the Gaeta, Picholine, and Bella di Cerignola at your local gourmet shop.

Olive Oil: Marcella Hazan, the famed Italian food authority, says that using anything but extra-virgin olive oil in salads is "inconceivable." Extra-virgin is the highest-quality oil you can buy. It comes from the first pressing of the olives and, as a result, has the most flavor. As with all ingredients in uncooked dishes, it is imperative to use the best quality you can, so all the recipes that follow specify extra-virgin olive oil. Olive oil gives an uncooked dish body that plain vegetable oil can't. But there are times when olive oil is inappropriate. Most mayonnaises, for example, require a more neutral oil that won't overpower what are supposed to be the dominant flavors. (Aïoli is the exception here.) In general, however, raw preparations are enhanced by the addition of olive oil. It is expensive, so I look for jugs of extra-virgin Bertolli brand at my local warehouse discount club. Olive oil keeps indefinitely, stored in its bottle in a cool, dry pantry.

Soy Sauce: Soy sauce is a staple in all kinds of Asian-inspired sauces and dressings. For everyday use, I find the Kikkoman brand, available in almost any supermarket, to be just fine.

Sun-dried Tomatoes: Sun-dried tomatoes are summer in a bottle. I use them in pestos, on sandwiches, and to garnish crostini and other kinds of canapés. Place loose sun-dried tomatoes in a heatproof bowl, cover with boiling water, and let stand until softened, about 30 minutes. Then drain the tomatoes, put them in an airtight container, cover with olive oil, and season with salt, pepper, and herbs to taste. Let stand at least overnight before using. For convenience, sun-dried tomatoes packed in extra-virgin olive oil can't be beat. Bring tomatoes to room temperature before using. Either type of tomato will keep for at least two months in the refrigerator.

Vinegar: Vinegar is indispensable to the cool kitchen. The three types of vinegar I use most often are red wine, balsamic, and sherry wine. Red wine vinegar has a straightforward acidic taste that perfectly complements good olive oil. Balsamic vinegar is sweeter and richer. Sherry wine vinegar tastes strongly of the fortified wine from which it is made. Each adds something different to a dish. Vinegars will keep indefinitely in a cool, dry place.

Wasabi Powder: Wasabi is Japanese horseradish, green in color and most familiar to Americans as a sushi condiment. It is available in Asian markets and many supermarkets in both powder and paste forms. I prefer the powder, which you mix with a little bit of water as needed, because it keeps well in a cool, dry pantry. Wasabi has bite—if you like a blast of flavor with your seafood, meat, or vegetables, you should give it a try.

Wine and Liquor: While developing these recipes, I was surprised to notice how many times I found myself raiding the liquor cabinet to add flavor and interest to my desserts. I keep tiny bottles of Grand Marnier, kirsch, framboise, rum, and brandy on hand to give fruit desserts an extra dimension. I rarely open a bottle of wine or Champagne just to use in a dessert, but if I have an open bottle around, I'll pour what's left over on top of fruit.

STARTERS AND SOUPS

- ❖ Five-Spice Nuts
- ❖ Raisin and Honey-Roasted Peanut Party Mix
- ❖ Marinated Green Olives with Lemon and Thyme
- ❖ Marinated Black Olives with Orange and Fennel
- ❖ Vodka-Spiked Cherry Tomatoes with Cumin-Cilantro Dipping Salt
- ❖ Prosciutto-Fig ''Sandwiches''
- ❖ Dates Stuffed with Garlicky Goat Cheese
- ❖ Goat Cheese Wrapped in Grape Leaves
- ❖ Explorateur and Berry Canapés
- ❖ Spicy Marinated Bocconcini
- ❖ Ricotta and Chive Spread
- ❖ Chunky Artichoke Heart Spread
- ❖ Avocado Dip with Chipotles and Lime
- ❖ Lemony White Bean Dip
- ❖ Roasted Red Pepper and Walnut Dip
- ❖ Salmon Roe and Pickled Ginger on Crispy Rice Crackers
- ❖ Smoked Salmon and Endive Tapas
- ❖ Cold Avocado-Tequila Soup
- ❖ Summer Minestrone
- ❖ Tzatziki Soup
- ❖ White Gazpacho
- ❖ Honeydew and White Wine Soup
- ❖ Anchovy Paste and Sun-dried Tomato Toasts

Right after she graduated from college, my youngest sister Stacey invited me over to her first apartment for dinner. When I arrived, I saw laid out on her simple coffee table a small log of goat cheese that she'd garnished with a few sprigs of fresh rosemary, a little basket of crackers, and five or six cocktail napkins spread out in a spiral. It was the napkins that got me: so civilized, so thoughtful. I was horrified. I had hosted my sisters and friends many times in my own first apartment, and all of those times I had forgotten the cocktail napkins!

No, I wasn't afraid that Martha Stewart would come and drag me away in handcuffs in the middle of the night. But the memory of my sister's garnished goat cheese and her napkins still makes me think about simple ways I can show hospitality, even when I can't or don't want to cook. There is nothing more delightful than a before-dinner nibble that is pretty, tasty, and

unusual. And as you will see in the following recipes, there is nothing simpler to prepare.

Instead of just serving plain peanuts, toss the nuts with five-spice powder or spike some cherry tomatoes with vodka to start the party. There are marinated olives, elegant finger foods, simple dips and spreads. Of course, none of these recipes requires any cooking. I hope this will encourage you to try a few, even if you usually just open a bag of chips and call it a day.

At the end of the chapter are a few recipes for cold soups, an alternative way to begin an evening of simple entertaining. A cold soup imparts an aura of elegance to any meal, even if the menu consists of grilled steak, green salad, and watermelon slices for dessert. Serve little bowls of Cold Avocado-Tequila Soup at your next chicken barbecue, and you'll see what I mean.

A note on serving sizes: For most of the recipes in this chapter, I've noted the quantity you'll end up with rather than how many people each recipe serves. For example, one recipe of Five-Spice Nuts yields 3 cups. This will give you enough to serve to 6 or 8 people with drinks before dinner. It wouldn't be enough to serve to a Super Bowl party of 20, but it would make a nice addition to a larger table of chips, dips, and finger foods for that party. So think about how many people you want to feed and what else, if anything, you'll be offering when calculating how much food you should prepare. ❖

Five-Spice Nuts

Chinese five-spice powder is one of the great kitchen time-savers. No mess, no fuss, just five spices—star anise, fennel, cinnamon, cloves, and pepper—perfectly blended and ready to use. Here I toss salted nuts (I like precious macadamia nuts, but peanuts are great, too) with a tablespoon of five-spice powder for an addictive snack.

1 pound salted macadamia nuts or salted peanuts

1 tablespoon five-spice powder

Combine the nuts and five-spice powder in a medium-size bowl. Stir with a spoon until the nuts are evenly coated. The nuts will keep at room temperature in an air-tight container for a week.

Makes 3 cups

Raisin and Honey-Roasted Peanut Party Mix

Whenever I go to my aunt's house for dinner, she has a pretty ceramic bowl filled with raisins and peanuts sitting on her counter for everyone to munch on. This is barely a recipe—just two simple ingredients tossed together. But her guests don't seem to complain—until they reach the bottom of the bowl. These raisins and peanuts also make a great take-along snack for hiking or the beach.

One 12-ounce can honey-roasted peanuts
1½ cups raisins (about 6 ounces)

Combine the nuts and raisins in a medium-size bowl. The party mix will keep at room temperature in an airtight container for 1 week.

Makes 4 cups

Marinated Green Olives with Lemon and Thyme

Marinated olives are great with drinks before dinner—tasty and a little salty, but not at all filling. I keep both green and black varieties in my refrigerator so I always have a little cocktail nibble on hand.

Zest from 1 large lemon, removed in ¼-inch-thick strands with a vegetable peeler and cut into 3-inch-long strips

½ pound green olives, such as Sicilian colossal

8 sprigs fresh thyme

2 large cloves garlic, thinly sliced

½ cup extra-virgin olive oil

Combine all the ingredients in a plastic container. Seal with an airtight cover and turn it several times to coat the olives with the oil. Marinate them overnight, turning once or twice. Marinated olives will keep in the refrigerator for 1 to 2 weeks. Bring them to room temperature before serving.

Makes 2 cups

Marinated Black Olives with Orange and Fennel

*F*ennel and orange is a traditional southern Italian combination. These olives pair up nicely with the lemony green ones on page 15.

Zest from 1 medium orange, removed in ¼-inch-thick strands with a vegetable peeler and cut into 3-inch-long strips

½ pound black olives, such as kalamata

1 teaspoon fennel seeds

1 teaspoon hot red pepper flakes

½ cup extra-virgin olive oil

Combine all the ingredients in a plastic container. Seal with an airtight cover and turn it several times to coat the olives with oil. Marinate them overnight, turning once or twice. Marinated olives will keep in the refrigerator for 1 to 2 weeks. Bring them to room temperature before serving.

Makes 2 cups

Vodka-Spiked Cherry Tomatoes with Cumin-Cilantro Dipping Salt

*I*n this recipe, cherry tomatoes are punctured in several places and then marinated in vodka so they can soak up a little alcohol. A cumin-flavored dipping salt is served on the side to complement the "drunken" tomatoes. This is an unusual nibble—light and tasty, and great with cold beers or dry vodka martinis.

1 pint ripe cherry tomatoes

⅔ cup vodka

1 tablespoon ground cumin

2 tablespoons salt

1 tablespoon finely chopped fresh cilantro leaves

1. Carefully puncture each cherry tomato in a half-dozen places with a toothpick. Place the tomatoes in a bowl and add the vodka. Marinate at room temperature, turning the tomatoes occasionally, for 2 to 3 hours.

2. Combine the cumin, salt, and cilantro in a small bowl. Drain off most of the vodka from the cherry tomatoes and place them in a serving bowl. (Reserve vodka for making Bloody Marys; the vodka already has a faint tomato flavor.) Serve the tomatoes alongside the dipping salt and with toothpicks.

Makes 2 cups

Prosciutto-Fig "Sandwiches"

Bite into a sweet dried fig and there's a delightful surprise—a tender morsel of silky prosciutto. I like to serve these sweet-salty treats with bowls of spiced nuts and marinated olives, instead of the usual hunk of cheese and basket of crackers.

12 dried Calmyrna figs

3 thin slices of prosciutto, cut crosswise into 4 pieces

Slice each fig almost in half. Fold a piece of prosciutto in half and put it in between the fig halves. Gently press the halves together to seal. The "sandwiches" can sit at room temperature for up to 2 hours before serving.

Makes 12 sandwiches

Dates Stuffed with Garlicky Goat Cheese

I'm always looking for surprising flavor combinations, and here's a great one—exotic dates and piquant cheese. These little bites are great palate teasers and disappear quickly from any cocktail party spread.

4 ounces fresh goat cheese, crumbled with a fork
1 small clove garlic, finely chopped
1 tablespoon finely chopped fresh basil leaves
16 dates, split in half lengthwise and pits removed

1. Combine the cheese, garlic, and basil in a small bowl. Mash with a fork until the ingredients are combined well.

2. Spoon a little cheese into the middle of each date and press lightly to seal. The stuffed dates may be refrigerated for up to 2 hours. Let them come to room temperature before serving.

Makes 16 hors d'oeuvres

Goat Cheese Wrapped in Grape Leaves

*G*rape leaves sound exotic, but they're actually sitting in jars on a shelf in your supermarket alongside mundane items such as pickles and olives. Somehow goat cheese seems so fresh and different sprinkled with mint and wrapped in a grape leaf. These appetizers are great finger food. The wrappers make them neat and easy to pick up. They can be served with drinks, or could even make up part of a Middle Eastern buffet.

6 large grape leaves packed in brine

One 6-ounce log fresh goat cheese, cut into 12 round slices

2 tablespoons finely chopped fresh mint leaves

1. Lift the grape leaves from the brine and pat them dry with paper towels. Cut the leaves in half from top to stem.

2. Place a round of goat cheese on top of each grape leaf half. Sprinkle each piece of cheese with ½ teaspoon mint. Wrap the cheese in the leaves, folding the sides over the cheese and tucking the ends underneath. Refrigerate the stuffed grape leaves for up to 3 hours. Let them come to room temperature before serving.

Makes 12 hors d'oeuvres

Explorateur and Berry Canapés

French triple-crème cheese is the richest, most buttery cheese in existence. When it's slathered on a bit of bread, topped with ripe berries, and preferably served with a glass of sparkling wine, it makes an elegant start to a party. It's also a rich beginning to, say, a light summer meal of cold poached chicken or salmon and a steamed vegetable salad.

3 ounces Explorateur (or other triple-crème cheese such as Camembert or St.-André)

Twelve ½-inch-thick baguette slices (about half a baguette)

1 cup fresh raspberries

Spread a little cheese on each baguette round. Top each piece of bread with 2 or 3 berries. Serve immediately.

Makes 12 hors d'oeuvres

Spicy Marinated Bocconcini

Bite-size mozzarella balls marinated in olive oil and herbs are another staple of the Italian antipasto table. Here, creamy bocconcini play off sweet fresh oregano and the bottled hot peppers that I always have on hand in the refrigerator.

1 pound bocconcini (or large piece of fresh mozzarella, cut into bite-size pieces)

4 bottled hot peppers, stemmed, seeded, and coarsely chopped

6 to 8 sprigs fresh oregano, or ½ teaspoon dried

¼ cup extra-virgin olive oil

¼ teaspoon salt, or to taste

Combine all the ingredients in a medium bowl. Cover the bowl in plastic wrap and refrigerate for at least 3 hours, stirring once or twice. The marinated bocconcini will keep in the refrigerator for 2 days.

Makes 3 cups

Ricotta and Chive Spread

*T*wo miles from my house in opposite directions are two different Italian delis that make their own ricotta cheese. So anywhere I go, I know I'm close to one of these great sources. This homestyle cheese is firmer, drier, and much more flavorful than the supermarket variety. Its dairy freshness is complemented by the addition of chopped chives and any other mixture of herbs I happen to have around. I spread this herbed cheese on bruschetta or garlic toasts when I want a mild but satisfying appetizer or snack. Supermarket ricotta cheese can be used here, but only if you drain the excess water from it: Line a small colander or strainer with a few layers of paper towels. Next, spread the cheese over the towels and let it drain until thickened and creamy, about 1 hour.

1 cup ricotta cheese

1 tablespoon finely chopped fresh chives

1 tablespoon finely chopped fresh herbs
(basil, mint, and/or parsley leaves)

¼ teaspoon salt, or to taste

Freshly ground black pepper

Stir together the cheese, chives, herbs, salt, and pepper in a medium-size bowl. The cheese mixture can be refrigerated for 2 to 3 hours before serving.

Makes 1 cup

Chunky Artichoke Heart Spread

*B*ottled artichokes that are puréed are great on garlic toasts, pita chips, or bagel chips. There's no filler here—no sour cream, yogurt, or cottage cheese—just one secret ingredient, anchovies. For all you fearful anchovy haters, I promise that the finished product doesn't taste like anchovies, but the anchovies make it indescribably delicious.

One 12-ounce jar marinated artichoke hearts, drained (about 1½ cups)

¼ cup extra-virgin olive oil

4 anchovy fillets, drained and coarsely chopped

¼ cup tightly packed fresh parsley or basil leaves

Place all the ingredients in the work bowl of a food processor. Pulse several times until the mixture is blended but still chunky, scraping down the sides of the bowl 3 or 4 times as necessary. Scrape the spread into a small bowl. It can be made 2 or 3 hours before serving, covered in plastic wrap, and kept at room temperature.

Makes 1½ cups

Avocado Dip with Chipotles and Lime

*C*hipotles are a smoky variety of chile, packed in adobo, a mixture of tomato sauce and spices. They are available in gourmet stores and many supermarkets. The chilies give this dip a fantastic flavor, very different from conventional guacamole. I love the dip with salty tortilla chips. It's also great on the side with quick quesadillas—flour tortillas with a little grated Cheddar or Monterey Jack and maybe a few sliced cherry tomatoes sprinkled on top, and then popped into a 350°F oven for 10 minutes.

1 ripe avocado (about ½ pound), peeled, pitted, and coarsely chopped

1 tablespoon lime juice

2 canned chipotle chilies in adobo, coarsely chopped

½ cup sour cream

¼ teaspoon salt, or to taste

1. Place the avocado, lime juice, chilies, and sour cream in the work bowl of a food processor. Process until smooth, scraping down the sides of the bowl as necessary.

2. Scrape the dip into a small bowl. Stir in the salt. The dip can be made 2 or 3 hours before serving, covered in plastic, and refrigerated.

Makes 1 cup

Lemony White Bean Dip

his simple spread is light enough to serve as a dip with raw vegetables, and yet substantial enough to become a vegetarian main course when spread on thick slices of grilled bread.

Two 15-ounce cans white beans, drained and rinsed

2 cloves garlic, coarsely chopped

1 cup tightly packed fresh parsley leaves

¼ cup lemon juice

¼ cup olive oil

½ teaspoon salt, or to taste

1. Place the beans, garlic, parsley, lemon juice, and oil in the work bowl of a food processor. Process until smooth, scraping down the sides of the bowl once or twice as necessary.

2. Scrape the mixture into a small bowl. Stir in the salt. The dip can be made 2 or 3 hours before serving, covered in plastic wrap, and kept at room temperature.

Makes 2 cups

Roasted Red Pepper and Walnut Dip

*T*his is an unusual but simple dip, great with raw vegetables, pita chips, or garlic toasts (see Garlic Toasts, page 65).

One 12-ounce jar roasted red peppers, drained

1 large clove garlic, peeled

½ cup walnuts

½ cup tightly packed fresh basil leaves

1 slice white bread, crust removed, shredded into 6 or 8 pieces

¼ teaspoon salt, or to taste

1. Place the peppers, garlic, walnuts, basil, and bread in the work bowl of a food processor. Process until the nuts are finely chopped and the mixture is smooth, scraping down the sides of the bowl once or twice as necessary.

2. Scrape the mixture into a small bowl. Stir in the salt. The dip can be made 2 or 3 hours before serving, covered in plastic wrap, and kept at room temperature.

Makes 1½ cups

Salmon Roe and Pickled Ginger on Crispy Rice Crackers

I don't believe in making sushi at home—leave that to the trained professionals. But no training is required to whip up these appetizers when you get a craving for the flavors of the sushi bar. Pickled ginger and wasabi powder can be found in the gourmet aisle of many supermarkets, as well as at Asian groceries. Go to your fish market for salmon roe. I buy Petrossian brand. At $10 for 3½ ounces, it's affordable caviar.

2 tablespoons wasabi powder

2 tablespoons water

24 rice crackers (not rice cakes), such as Kame brand

24 small (about the size of a penny or nickel) pieces of pickled ginger

One 3½-ounce jar best-quality salmon roe

1. Place the wasabi powder and water in a small bowl. Stir until smooth. Let the mixture stand 15 minutes to allow the flavor to develop.

2. Spread a thin layer of wasabi paste on each cracker. Top with a sliver of pickled ginger and ½ teaspoon of salmon roe. Serve immediately.

Makes 12 hors d'oeuvres

Smoked Salmon and Endive Tapas

*T*his typical Spanish tapa fulfills all my requirements for great party food: It's delectable, easy to make, and easy to eat.

2 ounces sliced smoked salmon, cut into ¼-inch dice

2 teaspoons lemon juice

2 teaspoons drained capers

12 small endive leaves, wiped clean with a paper towel

1. Combine the salmon, lemon juice, and capers in a small bowl.

2. Spoon a little bit of the salmon mixture into each endive leaf. The tapas may be refrigerated for 1 hour before serving.

Makes 12 hors d'oeuvres

Cold Avocado-Tequila Soup

Are you tired of the same old guacamole but still in love with avocados? This soup is a wonderful alternative. It's rich and refreshing at the same time—a wonderful way to begin a festive summer meal. The tequila gives the avocado purée a nice edge.

½ cup tightly packed fresh cilantro leaves

1 jalapeño pepper, stemmed, seeded, and coarsely chopped

½ cup lemon juice

¼ cup tequila

One 15-ounce can chicken broth, fat skimmed from top

2 ripe avocados (about 1 pound), peeled, pitted, and coarsely chopped

½ teaspoon salt, or to taste

4 lemon wedges (optional)

1 small tomato (optional), cut into ¼-inch dice

1. Place the cilantro and jalapeño in a blender or the work bowl of a food processor. Process until finely chopped, scraping down the sides of the bowl once or twice as necessary.

2. Add the lemon juice, tequila, chicken broth, avocados, and salt and process until smooth. Refrigerate the soup until it is well chilled, about 1 hour. (It can be refrigerated for up to 6 hours until ready to serve.)

3. Ladle the soup into 6 serving bowls and garnish each bowl with a lemon wedge and a tablespoon or two of chopped tomato, if desired. Serve immediately.

Makes 4 servings

Summer Minestrone

*T*his chilled spicy soup requires a little chopping, but not much else. Its confetti-like colors and fresh flavors are delightful on a hot day. It makes a great light appetizer; add one 12-ounce can of drained and rinsed navy beans, and it becomes a substantial meal. Crunchy croutons contrast nicely with the veggies, or serve bruschetta or garlic toasts on the side. Olive oil adds a little luxury.

6 large, ripe tomatoes (about 3 pounds), cored and cut into ¼-inch dice

1 jalapeño pepper, stemmed, seeded, and finely chopped

1 yellow bell pepper, cored, seeded, and cut into ¼-inch dice

6 cloves garlic, peeled and crushed

6 scallions, green and white parts, chopped

1 medium cucumber, peeled and cut into ¼-inch dice

2½ cups water

2 tablespoons red wine vinegar

½ teaspoon salt, or to taste

½ cup croutons

2 tablespoons extra-virgin olive oil

1. Combine the tomatoes, peppers, garlic, scallions, cucumber, water, and vinegar in a large bowl. Refrigerate the soup until it is well chilled, about 1 hour. (It can be refrigerated for up to 6 hours until ready to serve.)

2. Remove and discard the garlic. Stir in the salt.

3. Ladle the soup into 6 serving bowls. Sprinkle each bowl with croutons and drizzle with olive oil. Serve immediately.

Makes **6** servings

Tzatziki Soup

*T*zatziki is a garlicky yogurt dip often found on the Greek appetizer table. When thinned with water and then well chilled, it makes a sparkling soup. This is great in the summer, when you want to eat everything cold, but I also like it as a light starter to a hearty Mediterranean meal of, say, braised lamb shanks or short ribs. When I want to feel virtuously healthy, I eat this with a loaf of fresh bread and a lightly dressed salad.

1 medium cucumber, peeled, seeded, and grated

3 cups plain yogurt

1 clove garlic, finely chopped

Zest of 1 lemon, grated

¼ cup lemon juice

¼ cup tightly packed fresh mint leaves, finely chopped

2 tablespoons extra-virgin olive oil

1 cup water

½ teaspoon salt, or to taste

1. Combine the cucumber and yogurt in a medium-size bowl. Stir in the garlic, lemon zest and juice, mint, oil, water, and salt.

2. Refrigerate the soup until it is well chilled, about 1 hour. (It can be refrigerated for 2 to 3 hours until ready to serve.) Ladle the soup into 6 serving bowls. Serve immediately.

Makes 6 servings

White Gazpacho

*T*his cold soup is a classic of Spanish cuisine. Almonds give it a lovely richness, and the green grape garnish prevents it from being *too* rich. Make sure to use sherry wine vinegar. There's no substitute for the particularly Spanish flavor it imparts.

1 cup whole blanched almonds

3 cloves garlic, coarsely chopped

1½ cups stale Italian or French bread, crusts removed and torn into small pieces

3 cups ice water

¼ cup extra-virgin olive oil

1 tablespoon sherry wine vinegar

½ teaspoon salt, or to taste

1 cup seedless green grapes

1. Place the almonds, garlic, bread pieces, and 1 cup of the water in the work bowl of a food processor. Process until a smooth paste forms, scraping down the sides of the bowl 3 or 4 times as necessary.

2. With the motor running, add the oil in a slow stream. Add the remaining 2 cups water and process until smooth.

3. Scrape the mixture into a large bowl. Whisk in the vinegar and salt. Refrigerate the soup until it is well chilled, about 1 hour. (It can be refrigerated for up to 6 hours until ready to serve.)

4. Ladle the soup into 6 serving bowls. Garnish with the grapes. Serve immediately.

Makes **6** servings

Honeydew and White Wine Soup

*B*eginning a summer meal with this soup is like sipping a delicious fruit cocktail. It refreshes without spoiling your appetite. Depending on the sweetness of your melon, you might add more or less honey.

8 cups diced, chilled honeydew melon
   (about 1 large melon)
1 cup fruity white wine
3 tablespoons lime juice
3 teaspoons honey, or to taste
½ cup fresh raspberries

1. Place the honeydew, wine, lime juice, and honey in a blender. Puree until frothy. Refrigerate the soup until it is well chilled, about 1 hour. (It can be refrigerated for up to 6 hours until ready to serve.)

2. Stir the soup to redistribute any remaining foam. Ladle it into 4 soup bowls. Scatter a few berries on top of each bowl. Serve immediately.

Makes 4 servings

Anchovy Paste and Sun-dried Tomato Toasts

*U*se prepared toasts or crackers for these tasty appetizers, or use homemade Garlic Toasts (page 65). In the summer, some chopped fresh tomato can be substituted for the sun-dried tomatoes. Anchovy paste is available in many supermarkets, gourmet stores, and Italian specialty markets.

12 toasts or crackers

2 tablespoons anchovy paste

24 small sun-dried tomatoes packed in oil, drained, rinsed, and coarsely chopped

1 tablespoon chopped fresh parsley leaves

1 lemon wedge (⅛ of a lemon)

Spread each cracker with ½ teaspoon of anchovy paste. Top with the chopped sun-dried tomatoes. Sprinkle with parsley. When all of the canapes are assembled, squirt a few drops of lemon juice over each one. Serve immediately.

SALADS

- ❖ Lemony Fennel and Feta Salad
- ❖ Peach and Tomato Salad with Curry Vinaigrette
- ❖ Romaine Lettuce with Pecan-Gorgonzola Dressing
- ❖ Spinach Salad with Cucumber-Feta Dressing
- ❖ Minted Chickpea Salad
- ❖ Lima Bean, Ricotta Salata, and Basil Salad
- ❖ Bread Salad with Goat Cheese and Navy Beans
- ❖ Black-Eyed Pea and Smoked Ham Salad with Roasted Red Pepper Dressing
- ❖ Chicken and Jicama Salad with Ginger Vinaigrette
- ❖ Smoked Chicken Salad with Bulgur, Olives, Raisins, and Pine Nuts
- ❖ Taco Salad with Chicken and Black Beans
- ❖ Asian Scallop Seviche
- ❖ Baja Shrimp Salad with Avocado Dressing
- ❖ Grapefruit, Shrimp, and Arugula Salad
- ❖ Shrimp and Papaya Salad
- ❖ Crabmeat and Oranges over Frisée
- ❖ Fresh Tuna Niçoise Salad
- ❖ Mediterranean Tuna and Radish Salad
- ❖ Tuna, White Bean, and Escarole Salad
- ❖ Salmon on Romaine Lettuce with Chunky Avocado Dressing
- ❖ Panzanella with Mozzarella and Salami
- ❖ Roast Beef and Parmesan over Bitter Greens
- ❖ Chef's Salad with Serrano Ham and Manchego
- ❖ Prosciutto, Fig, and Melon Salad

I'll never forget making dinner for my sister Barri one night after a long day at work. This is a woman so uninterested in using her stove that she waited a year to have the gas turned on in her apartment. As she watched me grate Parmesan; wash romaine lettuce; shake up some olive oil, lemon juice, garlic, and chopped anchovies; and toss it all with crunchy croutons, she said with surprise, "I could do that!" I felt refreshed by her enthusiasm and by the simple food that seemed to appear before us without any work.

The recipes in this chapter are for everyone who loves salad but maybe patronizes the local salad bar too often. Healthy, quick, and full of interesting textures and flavors, no-cook salads are a refreshing alternative to pizza and take-out Chinese. In the same time it takes to order fast food and have it delivered, you can make a Tuna, White Bean, and Escarole Salad or Black-Eyed Pea and Smoked Ham Salad with Roasted Red Pepper Dressing.

Making your own salad allows you to control the quality of ingredients. It gives you a sense of accomplishment and creative satisfaction. Most important, making salad can satisfy all of your cravings for flavor in mere minutes. If you can shop and then chop, you can prepare a delicate fennel and feta salad to go with some pasta; you can dress cooked shrimp with avocado and lime juice for an appetizer that will take you right to the west coast of Mexico; or you can toss chicken and jicama with a piquant ginger vinaigrette for a satisfying one-dish meal. So get out your salad spinner, chef's knife, and oil and vinegar, and discover what you can do. ❖

Lemony Fennel and Feta Salad

When fennel and feta are combined, something happens—the fennel seems less sweet and the feta seems less salty. They turn out to be perfectly complementary. I serve this salad as a prelude to all kinds of meals. It's great served on the side with roasted chicken. It's also good with grilled squid or shrimp. And it's terrific before (or after—Italian-style) a bowl of pasta or a pizza with a simple tomato sauce without cheese.

1 medium fennel bulb

2 tablespoons lemon juice

2 tablespoons extra-virgin olive oil

3 ounces feta cheese, crumbled

Freshly ground black pepper, to taste

1. Cut off the stalks and feathery tops of the fennel bulb and trim away the tough outer leaves. Coarsely chop the feathery tops and set them aside. Quarter the bulb and cut each quarter lengthwise into very thin slices.

2. Combine the fennel, lemon juice, and olive oil in a large bowl. Arrange the dressed fennel on 4 salad plates. Top with the crumbled feta, freshly ground pepper, and chopped fennel fronds. Serve immediately.

Makes 4 servings as an appetizer;
2 servings as a main course

Peach and Tomato Salad with Curry Vinaigrette

*T*his might sound strange, but I promise there's nothing more taste tingling and refreshing than peaches, tomatoes, and curry. This is a great starter or side dish to a simple barbecue. Add this salad to a meal of corn and grilled burgers or flank steak for instant excitement.

¼ cup extra-virgin olive oil

1 tablespoon lemon juice

¼ teaspoon curry powder

¼ teaspoon salt, or to taste

1 tablespoon chopped fresh parsley leaves

2 large, ripe tomatoes, each cut into 8 wedges

2 ripe peaches, each pitted and cut into 8 wedges

1. Whisk together the oil, lemon juice, curry powder, salt, and parsley in a small bowl.

2. Arrange the tomatoes and peaches on 4 salad plates, alternating them so that they form a pinwheel in the center of the plate.

3. Drizzle the dressing over each plate. Serve immediately.

Makes 4 servings as an appetizer;
2 servings as a main course

Romaine Lettuce with Pecan-Gorgonzola Dressing

*S*ometimes all I want for lunch or even dinner is a green salad and some crusty bread. The dressing is rich and strong enough to make this "salad" seem like a main dish. Of course, you can serve this salad as a prelude to a more elaborate meal.

⅓ cup pecans

2 tablespoons lemon juice

½ cup plain yogurt

2 tablespoons extra-virgin olive oil

2 tablespoons finely chopped fresh parsley leaves

¼ pound gorgonzola, crumbled

¼ teaspoon salt, or to taste

1 medium head romaine lettuce, tough outer leaves discarded, usable leaves rinsed and torn into bite-size pieces

1. Place the pecans in the work bowl of a food processor. Process until coarsely chopped.

2. Add the lemon juice, yogurt, oil, parsley, and cheese and process until smooth. Scrape the dressing into a small bowl. Add the salt.

3. Toss the lettuce with the dressing in a large bowl. Divide the salad among 4 plates (or 2 plates if serving as a main course). Serve immediately.

Makes 4 servings as an appetizer;
2 servings as a main course

Spinach Salad with Cucumber-Feta Dressing

I'm always looking for new ways to dress tender raw spinach. This is a good one—cool cucumber and yogurt puréed with salty, tangy feta. If you want to serve this as a main course, add ¾ pound of cooked chicken or shrimp.

1 medium-size cucumber, peeled, seeded, and coarsely chopped

¼ pound feta cheese, crumbled

½ cup plain yogurt

2 tablespoons chopped chives

¼ teaspoon salt, or to taste

1 pound fresh spinach, stemmed, washed, and dried

2 medium tomatoes, each cored and cut into 8 wedges

1. Combine the cucumber, feta, and yogurt in the work bowl of a food processor. Process until smooth, scraping down the sides of the bowl once or twice as necessary. Transfer the dressing to a small bowl.

2. Stir the chives and salt into the dressing.

3. Combine the spinach, tomatoes, and the dressing in a large bowl. Toss until evenly coated. Divide the salad among 4 salad plates (or 2 if serving as a main course). Serve immediately.

Makes 4 servings as an appetizer;
2 servings as a main course

Minted Chickpea Salad

I **love chickpeas,** especially the canned organic ones that are so amazingly firm and flavorful. Here the chickpeas are tossed with abundant mint, crunchy cucumbers, and diced tomatoes. It's a colorful, tasty combination, whether you serve it as a vegetarian main course or on the side with chicken, steak, or lamb.

Two 15-ounce cans chickpeas (preferably organic), drained and rinsed

1 cup tightly packed fresh mint leaves, finely chopped

1 medium cucumber, peeled, quartered, and sliced into ¼-inch-thick pieces

1 medium tomato, cored and cut into ¼-inch dice

1 shallot, finely chopped

¼ cup lemon juice

¼ cup extra-virgin olive oil

¼ teaspoon salt, or to taste

Combine all the ingredients in a large bowl and gently toss until the chickpeas and cucumbers are well mixed and coated with oil and lemon juice. The chickpea salad, covered in plastic, can be refrigerated for up to 6 hours before serving.

Makes 6 servings as a side dish;
4 servings as a main course

Lima Bean, Ricotta Salata, and Basil Salad

Ricotta salata is made from fresh ricotta cheese that's been salted and dried. It's like feta cheese, but creamier and less salty. Imported from Italy, it's widely available in supermarkets and Italian delis. This salad is a great side dish, but also a great vegetarian main course, served with good bread and maybe some sliced ripe tomatoes sprinkled with basil.

Two 15-ounce cans lima beans, drained and rinsed
¼ pound ricotta salata, crumbled
1 cup tightly packed fresh basil leaves
¼ cup finely chopped red onion
¼ cup extra-virgin olive oil
1 tablespoon balsamic vinegar

Combine all the ingredients in a large bowl. The lima bean salad, covered in plastic, can be refrigerated for 2 to 3 hours before serving.

Makes 6 servings as an appetizer or side dish;
4 servings as a main course

Bread Salad with Goat Cheese and Navy Beans

I **started out** with a few of my favorite no-cook ingredients to create this bread salad, and in the end I think the whole is greater than the sum of its parts. The goat cheese partially dissolves into a creamy dressing, and watercress adds a little bite. The bread and beans give this salad the heft of a healthy but substantial one-dish meal.

3 tablespoons extra-virgin olive oil

1 tablespoon balsamic vinegar

1 small clove garlic, finely chopped

¼ teaspoon salt, or to taste

2 tablespoons finely chopped fresh mint leaves

3 large tomatoes, cored and cut into ¼-inch dice

*4 cups leftover country white bread,
   cut into ¼-inch cubes*

*One 15-ounce can navy beans (preferably organic),
   drained and rinsed*

4 ounces fresh goat cheese, crumbled

1 bunch watercress, stemmed, washed, and dried

Whisk together the oil, vinegar, garlic, salt, and mint in a small bowl. Combine the rest of the ingredients in a large bowl. Pour the dressing over the salad and toss well so that the bread absorbs the tomato juice and dressing. Serve immediately.

Makes 6 servings as an appetizer or side dish;
4 servings as a main course

Black-Eyed Pea and Smoked Ham Salad
with Roasted Red Pepper Dressing

Bottled roasted red peppers must be one of the all-time best convenience foods. I use them on sandwiches, in salads, and here in a delicious dressing for creamy black-eyed peas and smoky ham. Seek out a good gourmet deli where they roast their own ham and will slice it thick for you.

¼ cup extra-virgin olive oil

1 tablespoon red wine vinegar

1 cup bottled roasted red peppers, drained
  (about 6 ounces)

1 clove garlic, coarsely chopped

¼ teaspoon salt, or to taste

Two 15-ounce cans black-eyed peas, drained and rinsed

½ pound smoked ham, sliced ¼ inch thick and
  cut into ¼-inch dice

1 bunch arugula, stemmed, washed, and dried

Place the oil, vinegar, peppers, and garlic in the work bowl of a food processor. Process until smooth. Scrape the dressing into a small bowl and stir in the salt. Combine the peas, ham, and arugula in a large bowl. Toss with the dressing to coat. Serve immediately.

Makes 6 servings as a side dish;
4 servings as a main course

Chicken and Jicama Salad with Ginger Vinaigrette

*C*runchy jicama and spicy ginger perfectly complement white-meat chicken in this simple but unusual salad.

3 tablespoons extra-virgin olive oil

1 tablespoon Dijon mustard

Zest of 1 lemon, grated

1 tablespoon lemon juice

2 teaspoons finely chopped fresh ginger

2 tablespoons finely chopped fresh cilantro leaves

¼ teaspoon salt, or to taste

¾ pound cooked boneless, skinless chicken breast, cut into ¼-inch dice

2 cups peeled and chopped jicama, in ¼-inch dice

3 scallions, green and white parts, sliced into thin rounds

1 medium head Boston lettuce, washed and dried

Whisk together the oil, mustard, lemon zest and juice, ginger, cilantro, and salt in a small bowl. Combine the chicken, jicama, and scallions in a medium-size bowl. Toss with the dressing to coat. Divide the lettuce leaves among 4 salad plates. Top with the chicken salad. Serve immediately.

Makes 4 servings as a light main course

Smoked Chicken Salad with
Bulgur, Olives, Raisins, and Pine Nuts

This is a great no-cook dish. Bulgur, already steamed and dried, is just rehydrated and fluffed with a fork before serving. It provides just the right whole-grain background for the contrasting salty-sweet flavors of the chicken, olives, raisins, and pine nuts. Smoked chicken can be found at many gourmet stores and supermarkets. I buy a whole smoked breast and slice it myself. Smoked turkey from the deli counter can be substituted.

1 cup fine bulgur

1 cup water

2 tablespoons lemon juice

2 tablespoons extra-virgin olive oil

½ pound smoked chicken, shredded into bite-size pieces

12 green olives, pitted and coarsely chopped

¼ cup pine nuts

¼ cup raisins

2 tablespoons chopped fresh parsley leaves

¼ teaspoon salt, or to taste

1. Combine the bulgur, water, lemon juice, and olive oil in a medium bowl. Let the mixture sit until the liquid is absorbed, about 30 minutes, then fluff it with a fork.

2. Stir in the chicken, olives, pine nuts, raisins, parsley, and salt. The bulgur and chicken salad, covered in plastic, can be refrigerated for 2 to 3 hours before serving. Let the salad come to room temperature before serving.

Makes 4 servings as a main course

Taco Salad with Chicken and Black Beans

When my bread salads turned out to be such a hit, I started thinking about variations on the theme. In this successful experiment, I threw together tortilla chips with shredded chicken, black beans, hot sauce, and tomatoes. I didn't want my dish to resemble anything you might pick up at Taco Bell, so I was careful to keep the ingredients fresh and the flavors straightforward. See Making Your Own Corn Tortilla Chips (page 51) if you're interested in improving on America's favorite snack food.

¾ pound cooked boneless, skinless chicken breast,
 cut into ¼-inch dice

Two 15-ounce cans black beans (preferably organic),
 drained and rinsed

2 medium tomatoes (about ½ pound),
 cored and cut into ¼-inch dice

1 ripe avocado, peeled, pitted, and cut into ¼-inch dice

2 tablespoons lime juice

2 tablespoons extra-virgin olive oil

1 teaspoon hot sauce

½ teaspoon salt, or to taste

3 cups tortilla chips (about 4 ounces)

Lettuce leaves, for garnish (optional)

Combine the chicken, beans, tomatoes, avocado, lime juice, olive oil, hot sauce, and salt in a medium-size bowl. Stir in the chips so that they absorb a little bit of the liquid from the salad. If using lettuce, divide the leaves among 4 plates and spoon the salad on top. Serve immediately.

Makes 4 servings as a main course

MAKING YOUR OWN
CORN TORTILLA CHIPS

Making tortilla chips from supermarket corn tortillas requires very little effort. So I refuse to think of myself as obsessive for trying to improve on what has become the quintessential convenience snack. "Homemade" chips really are better—and they are lower in fat and salt than the supermarket brands. To make your own corn chips, cut the corn tortillas into wedges, spray them with vegetable oil spray, sprinkle them with salt if you like, and toast them in a 350°F oven for 10 to 15 minutes until they're crisp.

Other recipes for which "homemade" tortilla chips would be perfect:

- ❖ Avocado Dip with Chipotles and Lime (page 25)
- ❖ Lemony White Bean Dip (page 26)
- ❖ Cilantro Mojo (page 126)
- ❖ Jalapeño-Tomato Salsa (page 117)
- ❖ Jamaican Papaya and Avocado Relish (page 123)

Asian Scallop Seviche

*I*n this simple recipe, scallops are marinated in a lime juice mixture and then spooned over an Asian-flavored coleslaw. For safety's sake, as well as for flavor, always buy your scallops at a reputable fish market. If you want to add some carbohydrate heft, substitute cooked rice noodles for the cabbage (see Japanese Rice Noodles, page 56). It becomes a different dish, but just as interesting and satisfying.

1 pound bay or sea scallops, drained, blotted dry with paper towels, sea scallops cut into quarters

¼ cup lime juice

6 scallions, white and green parts, thinly sliced

1 small fresh red chili pepper or 1 jalapeño pepper, seeded and finely chopped

4 cups shredded green or napa cabbage

2 medium carrots, shredded with a vegetable peeler or in a food processor

2 teaspoons finely chopped fresh ginger

1 tablespoon finely chopped fresh cilantro leaves

2 tablespoons Asian sesame oil

¼ teaspoon salt, or to taste

1. Combine the scallops, lime juice, scallions, and chili pepper in a medium bowl. Cover with plastic and refrigerate for 2 to 2½ hours, until the scallops lose their translucence.

2. Combine the cabbage and carrots in a large bowl. Add the ginger, cilantro, sesame oil, and salt and toss until well combined.

3. Divide the coleslaw among 4 plates. Mound the scallops on top of each portion of coleslaw, and spoon the remaining marinade over each plate. Serve immediately.

Makes 4 main-course servings

Baja Shrimp Salad with Avocado Dressing

or me, nothing evokes the west coast of Mexico like this elemental combination of shrimp, avocado, and lime. Very good cooked shrimp can be found in the freezer case of your supermarket (see Frozen Shrimp, page 5). The salad, lettuce and all, can be wrapped in warm corn or flour tortillas.

1 ripe avocado, peeled, pitted, and cut into ¼-inch dice

1 small, ripe tomato, cored and cut into ¼-inch pieces

2 tablespoons chopped red onion

2 tablespoons extra-virgin olive oil

2 tablespoons lime juice

½ teaspoon salt, or to taste

12 ounces medium cooked shrimp, peeled

Green leaf lettuce, for garnish (optional)

Combine the avocado, tomato, onion, olive oil, lime juice, and salt in a small bowl. Arrange the shrimp (on top of lettuce, if you like) on 4 plates. Spoon the avocado mixture over each plate. Serve immediately.

Makes 4 servings as an appetizer;
2 servings as a main course

Grapefruit, Shrimp, and Arugula Salad

*I*n this salad, sweet grapefruit, rather than the same old squirt of lemon juice, brings out the flavor of cooked shrimp.

1 large pink or white grapefruit, peeled, sectioned, and cut into ¼-inch dice

¼ cup extra-virgin olive oil

2 tablespoons lemon juice

2 tablespoons finely chopped fresh basil leaves

1 clove garlic, finely chopped

¼ teaspoon salt, or to taste

1 pound cooked shrimp, peeled and cut into ¼-inch dice

2 small bunches arugula, stemmed, washed, and dried

1. Combine the grapefruit, olive oil, lemon juice, basil, garlic, and salt in a small bowl.

2. Combine the shrimp and arugula in a large bowl. Toss with the dressing. Divide the salad among 4 plates. Serve immediately.

Makes 6 servings as an appetizer; 4 servings as a light main course

Shrimp and Papaya Salad

I'm addicted to the sweet-hot combination of papaya and hot red pepper flakes in this recipe. Asian fish sauce, available in Asian markets and many supermarkets, gives the dressing its distinctive flavor and is a great alternative to soy sauce. I spoon this tropical salad over baby greens or rice noodles (see Japanese Rice Noodles, page 56).

1 clove garlic, finely chopped

¼ cup lemon juice

2 tablespoons fish sauce

½ teaspoon hot red pepper flakes

1 tablespoon sugar

2 medium-size papayas, halved, seeds scraped out and discarded, peeled, and cubed

1 pound small cooked shrimp, peeled

2 tablespoons chopped fresh cilantro leaves

Combine the garlic, lemon juice, fish sauce, red pepper flakes, and sugar in a small bowl. Stir to dissolve the sugar. Combine the papaya and shrimp in a medium-size bowl. Stir in the dressing and the chopped cilantro. Serve immediately.

Makes 6 servings as an appetizer;
4 servings as a light main course

JAPANESE RICE NOODLES

Japanese rice noodles, available at health food stores and Asian groceries, are practically a no-cook item. Simply place the noodles in a heatproof bowl, boil water, pour it over the noodles so that they are completely covered, and wait ten minutes. Drain the noodles and toss them with the topping of your choice. Eight ounces of uncooked noodles will serve four.

Aside from Shrimp and Papaya Salad, rice noodles would be great with:

❖ Asian Scallop Seviche (page 52)

❖ Indonesian Peanut Sauce (page 105)

❖ Orange-Ginger Dipping Sauce (page 104)

❖ Cucumber-Watermelon Salsa (page 122)

❖ Thai Dressing with Fish Sauce, Fresh Chilies, and Lime (page 103)

Crabmeat and Oranges over Frisée

This citrusy seafood salad is a luxurious treat. Crab and oranges might sound like a ladies' luncheon dish, but the curry in the dressing gives the salad a real kick. Other greens might be substituted, but the frisée, with its delicate, tickly leaves, catches every morsel of precious crab. Substitute cooked shrimp or lobster for the crab if you like.

⅓ cup extra-virgin olive oil

3 tablespoons lime juice

2 tablespoons finely chopped fresh basil leaves

½ teaspoon curry powder

¼ teaspoon cayenne pepper

¼ teaspoon salt, or to taste

¾ pound lump crabmeat

2 small navel oranges, peeled, sectioned, and cut into ½-inch dice

1 large or 2 small heads frisée, washed and dried

1. Whisk together the olive oil, lime juice, basil, curry powder, cayenne pepper, and salt in a small bowl.

2. Combine the crab, oranges, and lettuce in a large bowl. Pour the dressing over the salad and toss to coat. Serve immediately.

Makes 6 servings as an appetizer;
4 servings as a light main course

Fresh Tuna Niçoise Salad

I'm lucky to live in a place where I can buy sushi-quality tuna at my local fish market. If you're as lucky, you should try this simple but sophisticated salad.

3 tablespoons lemon juice

6 tablespoons extra-virgin olive oil

1 small clove garlic, finely chopped

¼ teaspoon salt, or to taste

1 medium head red or green leaf lettuce, washed, dried, and torn into pieces

10 ounces best-quality fresh tuna steak, cut across the grain into ⅛-inch-thick slices

12 ripe cherry tomatoes, quartered

4 teaspoons drained capers

¼ cup Niçoise olives, pitted and halved

4 anchovy fillets, drained and coarsely chopped

Freshly ground black pepper, to taste

1. Whisk together the lemon juice, olive oil, garlic, and salt in a small bowl.

2. Divide the lettuce among 4 salad plates. Next, arrange the tuna and tomatoes on top of the lettuce. Sprinkle each plate with some capers, olives, and anchovies.

3. Drizzle the dressing over each plate. Season with ground pepper. Serve immediately.

Makes 4 servings as an appetizer

Mediterranean Tuna and Radish Salad

*I*mported or domestic tuna packed in olive oil is a staple in my pantry. I make quick tomato sauces with it, use it on sandwiches, and especially in salads. This is a great main-dish salad, with tender tuna and crunchy, spicy radishes. Serve it on top of lettuce with crusty bread on the side for a substantial no-cook meal.

2 tablespoons lemon juice

3 tablespoons extra-virgin olive oil

¼ teaspoon salt, or to taste

1 pound radishes, thinly sliced

2 tablespoons chopped fresh parsley leaves

3 scallions, white and green parts, chopped

6 kalamata or other large black olives, pitted and coarsely chopped

Two 6-ounce cans tuna (preferably imported and packed in olive oil), drained and coarsely mashed with a fork

1 medium head romaine lettuce, washed, dried, and torn into bite-size pieces

1. Whisk together the lemon juice, olive oil, and salt in a small bowl.

2. Combine the radishes, parsley, scallions, olives, and tuna in a medium-size bowl. Pour the dressing over the salad and toss to coat.

3. Divide the lettuce leaves among 4 plates. Top with the tuna salad. Serve immediately.

Makes 4 servings as a main course

Tuna, White Bean, and Escarole Salad

*A*lthough the main components for this dish come right out of a can, this salad has a fine Italian pedigree and a simple elegance that will please any food snob. The croutons are not necessary but add some texture and bulk, or just serve some warm garlic bread on the side.

2 tablespoons red wine vinegar

¼ cup extra-virgin olive oil

1 small clove garlic, finely chopped

¼ teaspoon salt, or to taste

1 tablespoon finely chopped fresh parsley leaves

Two 6-ounce cans tuna (preferably imported and packed in olive oil), drained and coarsely mashed with a fork

One 12-ounce can white beans (preferably organic), drained and rinsed

1 medium head escarole, washed, dried, and torn into bite-size pieces

½ cup croutons (optional)

Whisk together the vinegar, olive oil, garlic, salt, and parsley in a small bowl. Combine the tuna, beans, escarole, and croutons in a large bowl. Gently toss the salad with the dressing. Serve immediately.

Makes 4 servings as a main course

Salmon on Romaine Lettuce with Chunky Avocado Dressing

*T*his delicious salad, made with some of my favorite ingredients—
sour cream, avocado, tomato, and garlic—works very well with canned
salmon. If you have the time, you might try poaching a salmon fillet
(see Poaching Salmon Fillets, page 62)—it's almost as easy as opening a can,
and it's a skill well worth acquiring.

1 ripe avocado, peeled, pitted, and cut into ¼-inch dice

2 tablespoons sour cream

2 tablespoons extra-virgin olive oil

¼ cup lime juice

2 tablespoons finely chopped fresh basil leaves

1 clove garlic, finely chopped

¼ teaspoon salt, or to taste

1 medium head romaine lettuce, washed, dried, and torn into bite-size pieces

2 medium tomatoes, each cut into 8 wedges

One 7½-ounce can salmon, drained and coarsely crumbled with a fork, or 1 poached salmon fillet (about ½ pound), coarsely mashed with a fork

½ cup croutons

1. Combine the avocado, sour cream, olive oil, lime juice, basil, garlic, and salt in a small bowl.

2. Combine the lettuce, tomatoes, salmon, and croutons in a large bowl. Toss with dressing until well coated. Divide the salad among 4 plates. Serve immediately.

Makes 4 servings as a main course

POACHING SALMON FILLETS

This is one of the easiest and most foolproof methods for cooking fish. If you try it, you will impress yourself with the results: perfectly cooked, moist fillets that any chef would be proud of. The secret is to turn off the heat as soon as you add the salmon to the water. The residual heat slowly cooks the fish so the fillets won't overcook or dry out.

Fill a large saucepan with enough water to cover your fillets. Bring the water to a boil. With a wide spatula, carefully place your fish in the pan, cover, and turn off the heat. Let the fish sit in the water for 30 minutes. Carefully remove it from the water, again with the wide spatula.

Poached salmon fillets are also great with:

❖ Basil Aïoli (page 107)

❖ Wasabi Mayonnaise (page 109)

❖ Hot Mustard and Sesame Dressing (page 102)

❖ Cilantro Mojo (page 126)

❖ Cucumber-Watermelon Salsa (page 122)

❖ Jamaican Papaya and Avocado Relish (page 123)

❖ Jalapeño-Tomato Salsa (page 117)

❖ Anchovy-Lemon Butter (page 106)

❖ Thai Dressing with Fish Sauce, Fresh Chilies, and Lime (page 103)

Panzanella with Mozzarella and Salami

*P*anzanella is Italy's solution to leftover bread. Day-old bread cubes are tossed with tomatoes and a vinaigrette to make a tasty and thrifty salad. I've added diced mozzarella and salami to make my salad a true main course. It's delicious—like an exploded Italian sandwich.

3 tablespoons extra-virgin olive oil

1 tablespoon red wine vinegar

1 small clove garlic, finely chopped

1 tablespoon fresh thyme leaves

3 large tomatoes, cored and cut into ¼-inch dice

1 tablespoon chopped chives

8 kalamata or other large black olives, pitted and coarsely chopped

4 cups diced leftover country white bread

1 bunch arugula, stemmed, washed, and dried

¼ pound fresh mozzarella, cut into ¼-inch dice

¼ pound spicy Italian-style salami, sliced ¼ inch thick, then cut into ¼-inch dice

Whisk together the olive oil, vinegar, and garlic in a small bowl. Combine the rest of the ingredients in a large bowl. Pour the dressing over the salad and toss well, so that the bread absorbs the tomato juice and dressing. Let it stand for 10 minutes, mixing once or twice. Serve immediately.

Makes 4 servings as a main course

Roast Beef and Parmesan over Bitter Greens

This salad, a take on the classic beef carpaccio, is a great prelude to a vegetarian pasta or risotto. I like to serve garlic toasts on the edge of each plate. Sometimes I'll make them myself (see Garlic Toasts, page 65) and other times I'll purchase the packaged ones sold at the deli counter of my supermarket.

¼ cup extra-virgin olive oil

4 teaspoons lemon juice

¼ teaspoon salt, or to taste

6 cups bitter greens (arugula, baby mustard, or turnip greens), washed and dried

½ pound rare roast beef, thinly sliced and cut lengthwise into 1-inch-wide strips

1 small (2 to 3 ounces) chunk Parmesan cheese

Freshly ground black pepper

16 small garlic toasts (optional)

1. Whisk together the olive oil, lemon juice, and salt in a small bowl.

2. Place the greens in a large mixing bowl and toss with the dressing.

3. Divide the dressed greens among 4 salad plates. Arrange the strips of roast beef in a circle on top of the greens. With a vegetable peeler, shave 8 or 10 Parmesan curls from the large hunk of cheese onto each plate. Season each plate with black pepper. Place 4 garlic toasts around the edge of each plate. Serve immediately.

Makes 4 servings as an appetizer

GARLIC TOASTS

Have half a stale baguette lying around? Take a few minutes to transform it into versatile toasts, which can accompany the Roast Beef and Parmesan over Bitter Greens (page 64) as well as many other salad, soup, and spread recipes in this book.

Slice half a baguette into ¼-inch-thick rounds. Finely chop 1 garlic clove. In a small bowl, combine the garlic with 2 tablespoons olive oil. Brush the bread rounds with oil on both sides. Place on a baking sheet and bake at 350°F for 10 minutes, turning once, until the rounds are golden and crisp. Cool the toasts and serve, or store them in an airtight container for up to 1 week.

Try homemade garlic toasts with:

❖ Summer Minestrone (page 31)

❖ Chunky Artichoke Heart Spread (page 24)

❖ Lemony White Bean Dip (page 26)

❖ Roasted Red Pepper and Walnut Dip (page 27)

❖ Ricotta and Chive Spread (page 23)

❖ Lemony Fennel and Feta Salad (page 40)

❖ Fresh Tuna Niçoise Salad (page 58)

❖ Chef's Salad with Serrano Ham and Manchego (page 66)

❖ Arugula Pesto (page 111)

❖ Olivada (page 112)

❖ Sun-dried Tomato and Black Olive Pesto (page 113)

Chef's Salad with Serrano Ham and Manchego

You know that diner-style chef's salad with slices of ham, turkey, hard-boiled egg, and American cheese, all arranged in a big glass bowl and covered in plastic? Well, forget about it. While this salad takes its name from that one, it gets its inspiration from delicious imported ham and cheese, and from the olives, roasted red peppers, and sherry wine vinegar often found in simple Spanish cooking.

¼ cup extra-virgin olive oil

1 tablespoon sherry wine vinegar

¼ teaspoon salt, or to taste

1 medium head green leaf lettuce (such as Boston or Bibb), washed, dried, and torn into bite-size pieces

¼ pound thinly sliced Serrano ham (or prosciutto)

¼ pound thinly sliced turkey breast

¼ pound Manchego cheese, coarsely crumbled

½ cup bottled roasted red peppers (about 3 ounces), cut into thin strips

8 black olives, pitted and coarsely chopped

Freshly ground black pepper to taste

1. Whisk together the olive oil, vinegar, and salt in a small bowl. Toss the greens with 3 tablespoons of the dressing in a large bowl.

2. Divide the lettuce among 4 large salad plates. Alternate slices of ham and turkey atop the lettuce. Sprinkle with the cheese and scatter the peppers and olives over the salads. Season with black pepper and drizzle the remaining dressing over each salad. Serve immediately.

Makes 4 servings as a main course

Prosciutto, Fig, and Melon Salad

*T*hese three special ingredients complement one another in this luxurious salad. It's a great fall treat when fresh figs and cantaloupe are available at the same time. Premixed greens are often available in the produce aisle of the supermarket; if they're not, just choose your favorites and mix.

½ small cantaloupe

4 cups mixed greens

4 ripe figs, cut into eighths

4 thin slices prosciutto, shredded

1 tablespoon lemon juice

3 tablespoons olive oil

1 teaspoon Dijon mustard

1 teaspoon honey

1 tablespoon mint, finely chopped

Salt and ground black pepper

1. Seed a melon half and cut into 4 wedges. Remove the rind from each wedge and cut into ⅛-inch wedges. Place the greens, melon, figs and prosciutto in a large bowl.

2. Combine the lemon juice, olive oil, mustard, honey, mint, and salt and pepper in a small bowl. Pour the dressing over the salad and toss to coat. Divide the salad among 4 salad platwqes. Serve immediately.

Makes 4 servings as a main course

SANDWICHES

- Walnut Butter and Apricot Jam Sandwiches
- Curried Chickpea Spread in a Pita
- Boston Lettuce and Maytag Blue Cheese Sandwich
- Cheddar and Apple Sandwiches with Honey Mustard
- Pears and Saint-André on Baguette
- Goat Cheese, Eggplant, and Roasted Red Pepper Sandwiches
- Herbed Goat Cheese and Sun-dried Tomatoes on a Bagel
- Smoked Mozzarella Sandwiches with Lemony Olives
- Mozzarella, Soppressata, and Artichoke Heart Sandwiches
- Chicken Caesar Salad Sandwich
- Chicken Salad Sandwich with Lemon-Herb Dressing
- Grilled Chicken Sandwiches with Mango Salsa
- Smoked Turkey, Fontina, and Arugula Sandwiches
- Smoked Chicken, Lettuce, and Tomato Sandwiches
- Turkey Sandwiches with Cranberry-Orange Relish
- Ham, Monterey Jack, and Chopped Hot Pepper Sandwiches
- Roast Beef and Rosemary Mushrooms on Focaccia
- Tuna, Cucumber, and Radish Sandwiches with Ginger Dressing
- Tuna and Salsa Verde Sandwiches
- Smoked Salmon and Cucumber Sandwiches with Dill Butter
- Smoked Salmon and Avocado Salad on a Bagel
- My Favorite Shrimp Salad Sandwich
- Lobster and Avocado Salad Sandwiches with Ginger-Lime Dressing
- Peanut Butter, Honey, and Peach Sandwiches

When I was in grade school, I used to open the sandwich that my Mom packed for me, eat whatever was inside, and throw away the squishy white bread. In college, I discovered fresh-baked bagels, decided these were a greater thing than sliced bread, and was happy to eat peanut butter on a bagel every day for lunch. In graduate school, I started making my own bread. After years of peanut butter on bagels, goat cheese on crusty white bread was a revelation. When I got a job working at Long Island's premier artisanal bakery, I reached the summit of my sandwich education. Every night I could take home what was left over from the day's production and match my daily loaf with a new filling. Sometimes it would be lemony chicken salad on eight-grain bread; sometimes it would be focaccia with rare roast beef; occasionally I would make a summer evening picnic of a baguette filled with ripe pears and triple-crème cheese. I haven't looked back.

When I began to write *Cool Kitchen*, I thought first of sandwiches—they are the original no-cook meal. I do not believe in cooking a lot of ingredients to put between two slices of bread; there's nothing more ridiculous than a sandwich that takes an hour to prepare. *Cool Kitchen* offers ideas that stay true to the spirit of the sandwich. There's nothing better than a Tuna and Salsa Verde Sandwich, unless it's a Ham, Monterey Jack, and Chopped Hot Pepper Sandwich. Or you might want to make a Walnut Butter and Apricot Jam Sandwich for the college student in you. It all depends on your mood and what you've got in the refrigerator.

A sandwich can only approach greatness if it is made lovingly with bread you can really sink your teeth into. Whether you're buying hot-dog buns, pitas, whole wheat bread, or buttery brioche, seek out the best sources for fresh and handmade loaves. Bread stays fresh in the freezer for up to one month if wrapped tightly in plastic and then in aluminum foil. ❖

Walnut Butter and Apricot Jam Sandwiches

Y ou can probably tell by my sweet tooth that I'm a former pastry chef. When I feel like eating lunch and dessert at the same time, I spread some homemade walnut butter and apricot jam on whole wheat bread. Homemade nut butters are easy and unusual—try grinding pecans or hazelnuts in the food processor, too. Use them the way you would peanut butter.

1¾ cups walnut pieces (about 6 ounces)
½ teaspoon brown sugar
Pinch of salt
8 slices whole wheat bread
¼ cup apricot jam (or other jam)

1. Place the walnuts, brown sugar, and salt in the work bowl of a food processor. Process until a smooth paste forms, scraping down the sides of the bowl once or twice as necessary.

2. Spread the walnut butter on 4 slices of bread. Spread the jam on the remaining 4 slices. Cover the walnut butter slices with the jam slices to make the sandwiches.

Makes 4 sandwiches

Curried Chickpea Spread in a Pita

*T*his is a lighter alternative to store-bought hummus, with a lot less added fat. Stuffing the chickpea-slathered pita with crisp salad ingredients makes the sandwich extra fresh-tasting. This chickpea spread is also great as a dip for pita chips or raw vegetables.

One 15-ounce can chickpeas, drained and rinsed

2 tablespoons extra-virgin olive oil

1 tablespoon lemon juice

¼ teaspoon curry powder

¼ cup tightly packed fresh cilantro leaves

¼ teaspoon salt, or to taste

4 pita breads, sliced three-quarters of the way around

4 romaine lettuce leaves, torn into bite-size pieces

1 large tomato, sliced

½ medium cucumber, peeled and sliced into ¼-inch-thick rounds

1. Place the chickpeas, olive oil, lemon juice, curry powder, and cilantro in the work bowl of a food processor. Process until smooth, scraping down the sides of the bowl once or twice as necessary. Scrape the mixture into a small bowl and stir in the salt.

2. Spread some chickpea paste on the bottom half of each pita, then put some lettuce, tomato, and cucumber into each one.

Makes 4 sandwiches

Boston Lettuce and Maytag Blue Cheese Sandwich

This is an all-American combination: Boston lettuce and Maytag Blue cheese. The mild lettuce in a lemony dressing makes a nice bed for this pungent cheese by cutting through its richness and complementing its strong flavor.

½ medium-size head Boston lettuce, washed, dried, and torn into small pieces

2 tablespoons extra-virgin olive oil

1 tablespoon lemon juice

⅛ teaspoon salt, or to taste

8 slices country white bread

4 ounces mild blue cheese (such as Maytag Blue), crumbled

Combine the lettuce, olive oil, lemon juice, and salt in a medium-size bowl. Divide the lettuce among 4 slices of bread. Sprinkle with the crumbled cheese. Finish with the remaining slices of bread.

Makes 4 sandwiches

Cheddar and Apple Sandwiches with Honey Mustard

Here's a healthy and homey cheese lover's sandwich. Tangy Cheddar cheese plays off the crunch of apple (try a tart variety like Granny Smith or McIntosh) and the sweet heat of honey mustard. I'm not an indiscriminate lover of bean sprouts, but they make sense here. The rich apple-Cheddar-honey mustard combination needs the lightening touch of some delicate green sprouts.

4 tablespoons honey mustard

8 slices country white bread

1 apple, cored and sliced into ⅓-inch-thick wedges

½ cup tightly packed bean sprouts

6 ounces extra-sharp Cheddar cheese, cut into ⅜-inch-thick pieces

Spread a tablespoon of mustard on each of 4 slices of bread. Top each slice with some apple, sprouts, and cheese. Finish with the final 4 slices of bread.

Makes 4 sandwiches

Pears and Saint-André on Baguette

*I*t's amazing how a few simple ingredients can transport you out of the supermarket right to a picnic in the French countryside. Lightly dressed lettuce contrasts well with the sweet fruit and creamy cheese. This is a great quick sandwich, and it travels well if you want to take lunch to work. If you're eating alone, substitute a crusty roll, use only two ounces of cheese, and eat the rest of the pear for dessert. Brie or Camembert can be substituted for the Saint-André.

1 small bunch frisée or arugula, stems trimmed, washed and dried

1 tablespoon lemon juice

2 tablespoons extra-virgin olive oil

¼ teaspoon salt, or to taste

1 crusty French baguette (16–20 inches), sliced in half lengthwise

1 ripe pear, halved, cored, and cut into ¼-inch-thick slices

½ pound Saint-André, rind removed and cut into ¼-inch-thick slices

Combine the lettuce, lemon juice, olive oil, and salt in a medium-size bowl. Arrange the dressed lettuce on the bottom half of the baguette. Top with the pear slices and then the cheese. Finish with the top half of the baguette. Slice the filled loaf into 4 equal sandwiches.

Makes 4 sandwiches

Goat Cheese, Eggplant, and Roasted Red Pepper Sandwiches

*I*n this Italian deli special, piquant goat cheese contrasts nicely with the creamy eggplant and sweet peppers. Bottled vegetables (look for eggplant and peppers imported from Italy) make a surprisingly fresh-tasting sandwich, especially with the addition of bright green basil dressing.

2 tablespoons extra-virgin olive oil

1 tablespoon red wine vinegar

1 small clove garlic, finely chopped

2 tablespoons finely chopped fresh basil leaves

¼ teaspoon salt, or to taste

*½ cup bottled marinated eggplant (about 4 ounces),
  coarsely chopped*

*½ cup bottled roasted red peppers (about 4 ounces),
  coarsely chopped*

6 ounces fresh goat cheese

4 crusty Italian rolls, sliced in half

1. Whisk together the olive oil, vinegar, garlic, basil, and salt in a small bowl. Combine the eggplant and peppers in a medium-size bowl. Toss with the dressing to coat.

2. Spread some goat cheese on the bottom half of each roll. Top with the eggplant and pepper mixture. Finish with the top halves of the rolls.

Makes 4 sandwiches

Herbed Goat Cheese and Sun-dried Tomatoes on a Bagel

I love bagels. There's something so basic about them. There have been years—the college years—when I've actually lived on bagels. Here I've replaced traditional cream cheese for a combination of goat cheese and sun-dried tomatoes. A little more elevated, but still the basic kind of sandwich I could lunch on every day for a long, long time.

6 ounces fresh goat cheese

1 tablespoon finely chopped fresh parsley, basil, or mint leaves

4 bagels, sliced in half

8 sun-dried tomatoes packed in oil, drained on paper towels, patted dry, and sliced into ¼-inch strips

Place the cheese and herbs in a small bowl. Mash with a fork to combine. Spread a little bit of cheese on each bagel half. Top with several sun-dried tomato slivers. Serve the sandwiches open-faced.

Makes 4 sandwiches

Smoked Mozzarella Sandwiches with Lemony Olives

*G*reen olives mixed with lemon zest are used in this sandwich to complement the creamy, smoky cheese.

Zest from 1 lemon, finely grated

12 green olives, pitted and coarsely chopped

2 tablespoons extra-virgin olive oil

1 baguette (16–20 inches), or 4 crusty rolls, sliced in half

6 ounces smoked mozzarella, cut into ¼-inch-thick slices

Combine the zest, olives, and olive oil in a small bowl. Spread a little of the olive mixture on the bottom half of the baguette or each roll. Top with the cheese and finish with the remaining bread. If using a baguette, slice the sandwich into 4 equal portions.

Makes 4 sandwiches

Mozzarella, Soppressata, and Artichoke Heart Sandwiches

A crusty roll, moistened with a little oil and vinegar, is topped with fresh mozzarella, spicy salami, and tender artichoke hearts. One stop at your local Italian deli and you've got the ingredients for a great sandwich that packs very well for picnics, hikes, and any other excursion.

2 tablespoons extra-virgin olive oil

1 tablespoon red wine vinegar

4 crusty Italian rolls, sliced in half

½ pound fresh mozzarella, cut into ¼-inch slices

¼ pound soppressata (or other spicy salami), thinly sliced

¼ cup (about 3 ounces) bottled marinated artichoke hearts, drained, patted dry, and cut into ¼-inch-thick pieces

Drizzle a little olive oil and vinegar over the bottom half of each roll. Top the rolls with slices of mozzarella, soppressata, and artichokes. Finish with the top halves of the rolls.

Makes 4 sandwiches

Chicken Caesar Salad Sandwich

favorite salad turns into a great sandwich when crusty rolls replace the traditional croutons. I like to put thin grilled chicken cutlets on this sandwich. (I go to a local deli where they sell fresh-cooked Bell & Evans, one of my favorite brands.) If you can't get cooked chicken cutlets, cut cooked whole chicken breasts into bite-size pieces.

4 tablespoons extra-virgin olive oil

2 tablespoons lemon juice

1 clove garlic, coarsely chopped

4 anchovy fillets, drained and coarsely chopped (optional)

½ small head romaine lettuce, torn into bite-size pieces

¼ cup grated Parmesan cheese

4 crusty Italian rolls, cut in half

1 pound grilled or sautéed boneless, skinless chicken cutlets

1. Place the olive oil, lemon juice, garlic, and anchovies in the work bowl of a food processor. Process until smooth, scraping down the sides of the bowl once or twice as necessary.

2. Combine the lettuce, dressing, and cheese in a medium-size bowl.

3. Divide the dressed greens among the bottom halves of the rolls. Top with the chicken cutlets and the remaining bread.

Makes 4 sandwiches

Chicken Salad Sandwich with Lemon-Herb Dressing

Here's a light and classic combination of chicken, lemon, and dill. I like the way chewy multigrain bread complements the chicken, but you could also give the salad some crunch by adding chopped celery.

¼ cup mayonnaise

¼ cup plain yogurt

1 tablespoon chopped fresh dill

½ teaspoon grated lemon zest

2 teaspoons lemon juice

¼ teaspoon salt, or to taste

2 cooked whole boneless, skinless chicken breasts
    (about 1 pound), cut into ¼-inch dice

4 lettuce leaves, for garnish (optional)

8 slices multigrain bread

1. Combine the mayonnaise, yogurt, dill, lemon zest and juice, and salt in a medium-size bowl. Add the chicken pieces. Toss with the dressing.

2. Place the lettuce leaves on 4 slices of bread, if desired. Divide the dressed chicken among the 4 slices. Top with the remaining bread.

Makes 4 sandwiches

HOW TO POACH BONELESS, SKINLESS CHICKEN BREASTS

If you can boil water, you can poach a chicken breast.

In a large skillet, bring 2 cups of water and 1½ teaspoons of salt to a boil. Lower the heat to a simmer and add 2 whole boneless, skinless chicken breasts. Cover and cook at a bare simmer for 5 minutes. Turn the chicken, cover, and cook for another 5 minutes. Remove the skillet from the heat, uncover, and let the chicken stand in the poaching liquid for 30 minutes. Remove the chicken from the water, put in an airtight plastic container, and refrigerate for up to 24 hours, until ready to use.

Recipes for which you can use poached chicken breasts:

- ❖ Chicken Salad Sandwich with Lemon-Herb Dressing (page 82)
- ❖ Chicken Caesar Salad Sandwich (page 81)
- ❖ Chicken and Jicama Salad with Ginger Vinaigrette (page 48)
- ❖ Taco Salad with Chicken and Black Beans (page 50)
- ❖ Arugula Pesto (page 111)
- ❖ Coconut Chutney (page 127)
- ❖ Indonesian Peanut Sauce (page 105)
- ❖ Orange-Ginger Dipping Sauce (page 104)

Grilled Chicken Sandwiches with Mango Salsa

Once you know how to peel a mango (see How to Peel a Mango, page 85), you'll want to use this delicious fruit in as many ways as possible—here's one of my favorites. Grilled chicken goes with this spicy-sweet salsa as naturally as peanut butter and jelly.

1 ripe mango, peeled and cut into ⅛-inch dice

2 tablespoons lime juice

2 tablespoons orange juice

1 jalapeño pepper, seeded and finely chopped

4 romaine lettuce leaves

1 grilled whole boneless, skinless chicken breast, cut into ¼-inch-thick slices

1 baguette (16–20 inches), sliced lengthwise

1. Combine the mango, lime juice, orange juice, and jalapeño in a small bowl. Let the salsa stand for 15 minutes to allow the flavors to develop, stirring once or twice.

2. Arrange the lettuce leaves on the bottom half of the baguette. Spoon the salsa over the lettuce. Top with the chicken slices and the remaining bread. Slice the filled loaf into 4 equal pieces.

Makes 4 sandwiches

HOW TO PEEL A MANGO

I learned how to peel a mango under the most difficult conditions. When I apprenticed with a French chef, he gave me a knife, a cutting board, a case of mangoes, and a warning: If you waste any of this precious fruit, don't come back to work tomorrow! But don't stress out. I know there are lots of fancy ways to separate the fruit from the pit, but this is the easiest.

Hold the mango in one hand, resting the stem end on the cutting board. With a sharp knife in the other hand, remove strips of skin, top to bottom, working around the fruit until all the skin is removed. Cut the flesh from the pit, again slicing from top to bottom, cutting all the way around the pit. Then, either slice into thin strips or dice.

Other mango recipes you'll want to try are:

❖ Tropical Fruit with Lime and Ginger (page 138)

❖ Melon and Mango with Yogurt "Crème Fraîche" (page 145)

Smoked Turkey, Fontina, and Arugula Sandwiches

*I*talian fontina is the perfect cheese for sandwiches. Mild but not boring, it pairs up perfectly with a variety of partners—prosciutto, olive paste, tomatoes. It's worth searching for in a cheese shop, gourmet store, or good Italian deli. Here I match it with smoked turkey and arugula—simple and delicious. Avoid domestic fontina and fontina imported from Denmark. They are waxy, tasteless cheeses that bear no resemblance to the original.

1 small bunch arugula, stemmed, washed, dried, and coarsely chopped

1 tablespoon extra-virgin olive oil

1 baguette (16–20 inches) or loaf Italian bread, split lengthwise

¾ pound sliced smoked turkey

⅓ pound Italian fontina cheese, cut into ¼-inch-thick slices

Toss the arugula with the olive oil in a medium-size bowl. Place the arugula on the bottom half of the baguette. Top with the turkey and then with the cheese. Finish with the top half of the baguette. Slice the filled loaf into 4 equal portions.

Makes 4 sandwiches

Smoked Chicken, Lettuce, and Tomato Sandwiches

When I get a craving for a BLT, but don't feel like frying bacon, I fix this sandwich. The smoked chicken is less fatty than pork. Arugula adds spice as well as crunch and the basil mayonnaise is a nice touch.

1 tablespoon finely chopped fresh basil leaves

¼ cup mayonnaise (preferably low-fat)

8 slices country white or whole wheat bread

12 arugula leaves, stemmed, washed and dried

1 large tomato, cut into 8 slices

½ pound sliced smoked chicken breast

Combine the basil and mayonnaise in a small bowl. Spread a tablespoon of basil mayonnaise on each of 4 slices of bread. Top each slice with 3 arugula leaves and 2 slices of tomato. Finish with the chicken and top with the remaining bread.

Makes 4 sandwiches

Turkey Sandwiches with Cranberry-Orange Relish

*T*his relish is great on that leftover Thanksgiving turkey (I actually serve it at the Thanksgiving table the first time around), but don't try it just once a year. Put together these festive sandwiches whenever you want to give thanks for the excellent store-roasted turkey breast available at local markets.

1 cup fresh or defrosted frozen cranberries (about 4 ounces)

2 tablespoons finely chopped red onion

¼ teaspoon hot red pepper flakes

2 teaspoons lime juice

1 navel orange, peeled, sectioned, and cut into ¼-inch dice

2 teaspoons finely chopped fresh ginger

2 tablespoons sugar

¼ cup coarsely chopped pecans

1 pound sliced turkey

8 slices rye bread

1. Place the cranberries in the work bowl of a food processor. Pulse several times until they are coarsely chopped.

2. Scrape the cranberries into a small bowl and stir in the onion, red pepper flakes, lime juice, orange, ginger, sugar, and pecans. Refrigerate the relish for 1 hour until well chilled.

3. Pile the turkey on 4 slices of bread. Top with the relish and then with the remaining bread.

Makes 4 sandwiches

Ham, Monterey Jack, and Chopped Hot Pepper Sandwiches

ere's a spicy variation on plain old ham and cheese. A little fresh cilantro mixed with bottled peppers adds a great kick.

6 or 7 bottled Italian hot peppers, stemmed, seeded, and coarsely chopped

2 tablespoons chopped fresh cilantro leaves

4 crusty rolls or 1 baguette, sliced in half

½ pound sliced Virginia ham

½ pound Monterey Jack cheese, cut into ¼-inch-thick pieces

1. Combine the peppers and cilantro in a small bowl.

2. Spread the pepper mixture on the bottom half of each roll or baguette.

3. Top with slices of ham and then cheese. Finish with the top halves of rolls or baguette. If using a baguette, slice the filled loaf into 4 equal pieces.

Makes 4 sandwiches

Roast Beef and Rosemary Mushrooms on Focaccia

*N*othing could be more satisfying than rare roast beef sandwiched between slices of fresh focaccia bread that's been scattered with thinly sliced raw mushrooms, olive oil, and garlic. Focaccia is an Italian flatbread—kind of like pizza without the topping. It's available at many Italian bakeries and delis, but if you can't find it, substitute any other good Italian bread.

1 cup stemmed and very thinly sliced fresh mushrooms (about 3 ounces)

3 tablespoons extra-virgin olive oil

2 teaspoons red wine vinegar

1 small clove garlic, finely chopped

1 teaspoon finely chopped fresh rosemary, or ½ teaspoon dried rosemary

¼ teaspoon salt, or to taste

One 8×8-inch focaccia bread, cut into 4×4-inch pieces and each piece sliced in half

1 pound sliced rare roast beef

1. Combine the mushrooms, olive oil, vinegar, garlic, rosemary, and salt in a small bowl.

2. Scatter the dressed mushrooms on the bottom halves of the bread. Top with the roast beef and finish with the remaining bread.

Makes 4 sandwiches

Tuna, Cucumber, and Radish Sandwiches with Ginger Dressing

I like tuna sandwiches with a little crunch, but I don't always want to use celery. Here's an alternative that's made with cucumber and radish.

Two 6-ounce cans tuna, drained

3 tablespoons canola oil

2 tablespoons rice vinegar

2 teaspoons peeled and finely chopped fresh ginger

4 scallions, white and green parts, cut into ¼-inch-thick rounds

½ medium-size cucumber, peeled, quartered, and thinly sliced

4 radishes, washed, trimmed, and cut into thin rounds

8 slices fresh white bread

Combine the tuna, oil, vinegar, ginger, scallions, cucumber, and radishes in a medium-size bowl. Divide the tuna salad among 4 pieces of bread. Top with the remaining bread.

Makes 4 sandwiches

Tuna and Salsa Verde Sandwiches

When **I was a student** living in Florence, I used to frequent an elegant little sandwich stand where well-heeled patrons would order at the counter and stand around on the cobblestone pedestrian walkway, munching their panini and sipping glasses of wine. I'd often just repeat the order of the person ahead of me and see what I would get. That's how I discovered one of my favorites—tuna with salsa verde, a bright green sauce made with parsley, garlic, anchovies, and capers.

½ cup tightly packed fresh parsley leaves

1 small clove garlic, peeled

1 tablespoon drained capers

2 anchovy fillets, drained

2 tablespoons lemon juice

¼ cup extra-virgin olive oil

4 crusty rolls, sliced in half

Two 6-ounce cans tuna, drained and coarsely mashed with a fork

1. Place the parsley, garlic, capers, anchovies, and lemon juice in the work bowl of a food processor. Process until coarsely chopped, scraping down the sides of the bowl once or twice as necessary. With the motor running, pour the oil through the feed tube until the ingredients become a smooth sauce.

2. Spread about 1 tablespoon of the sauce on the bottom halves of the rolls. Top with the tuna and the remaining halves of rolls.

Makes 4 sandwiches

Smoked Salmon and Cucumber Sandwiches with Dill Butter

ere is a classic combination of flavors and textures—silky salmon, sprightly dill, crunchy cucumber, earthy pumpernickel—that can't be improved upon. I serve these sandwiches open-faced so that the bread doesn't overwhelm the filling. For great hors d'oeuvres, remove the crusts and cut the sandwiches into 1-inch squares.

2 tablespoons butter, at room temperature

1 tablespoon finely chopped fresh dill

8 slices pumpernickel bread

*½ medium-size cucumber, peeled and cut into
⅛-inch-thick rounds*

½ pound thinly sliced smoked salmon

1. Combine the butter and dill in a small bowl, mashing with a fork until the butter is soft and the dill is evenly distributed.

2. Spread some dill butter on each slice of bread. Place the cucumber slices on top of the butter, pressing lightly to keep them in place. Top with the salmon. Serve open-faced.

Makes 4 sandwiches

Smoked Salmon and Avocado Salad on a Bagel

I love smoked salmon on a bagel. Sometimes I like to match it with creamy avocado instead of cream cheese for a change. I remove some of the bagel insides so that the salmon salad stays in place.

1 ripe avocado, peeled, pitted, and cut into ¼-inch dice

2 tablespoons finely chopped red onion

1 small tomato, cut into ¼-inch dice

1 tablespoon lemon juice

4 ounces thinly sliced smoked salmon, coarsely chopped

4 bagels, sliced and hollowed out

Combine the avocado, onion, tomato, lemon juice, and salmon in a small bowl. Spoon the salad into 4 bagel halves and top with the remaining halves.

Makes 4 sandwiches

My Favorite Shrimp Salad Sandwich

*T*his is one of my favorite ways to dress cooked shrimp for a sandwich. The briny anchovy dressing complements the sweetness of the shrimp. Fresh mint and lemon juice make the salad sparkle. I like this shrimp salad on crusty rolls, but pita pockets hold the loose shrimp and make an easy-to-eat sandwich.

1 clove garlic, coarsely chopped

4 anchovy fillets, drained and coarsely chopped

½ cup tightly packed fresh mint leaves

3 tablespoons extra-virgin olive oil

2 tablespoons lemon juice

⅛ teaspoon salt, or to taste

1 pound cooked shrimp, peeled and coarsely chopped

4 leaves sturdy lettuce (romaine, green leaf, Bibb, Boston)

4 rolls, cut in half, or 4 pita pockets, slit open halfway

1. Place the garlic, anchovies, and mint in the work bowl of a food processor. Process until coarsely chopped, scraping down the sides of the bowl several times as necessary. With the motor running, add the olive oil and lemon juice and process until smooth, again scraping down the sides of the bowl once or twice as necessary. Scrape the dressing into a small bowl and stir in the salt.

2. Combine the shrimp and the dressing in a medium-size bowl, tossing to coat. Place a lettuce leaf on the bottom half of each roll or pita. Spoon the shrimp over the lettuce and top with the remaining bread.

Makes 4 sandwiches

Lobster and Avocado Salad Sandwiches
with Ginger-Lime Dressing

*M*y local fish market sells cooked, shelled lobster meat. It's expensive, but every once in a while I'll indulge and turn out this simple but luxurious sandwich. I like fresh, soft white bread here—nothing too crunchy to obscure the toothsome lobster meat. On eastern Long Island, there's a fish shack famous for its lobster rolls, which are served on hot dog buns—also perfect for holding this crumbly salad.

½ pound cooked lobster meat (approximately two 1½-pound lobsters), cut into ⅛-inch dice

1 small avocado, peeled, pitted, and cut into ⅛-inch dice

2 tablespoons extra-virgin olive oil

2 tablespoons lime juice

2 teaspoons peeled and finely chopped fresh ginger

¼ teaspoon salt, or to taste

8 slices white bread or 4 hot dog buns

Combine the lobster, avocado, olive oil, lime juice, and ginger in a medium-size bowl. Stir in the salt. Divide the lobster salad among 4 pieces of bread. Top with the remaining bread.

Makes 4 sandwiches

Peanut Butter, Honey, and Peach Sandwiches

*T*his quick sandwich is a late-summer treat. In the winter, substitute ¼ cup raisins or other chopped dried fruit for the peach.

8 slices bread

½ cup peanut butter

1 peach, pitted, halved, and each half cut into 4 slices

4 teaspoons honey

Spread 4 slices of bread with 2 tablespoons of peanut butter each. Place 2 peach slices on top of each piece. Spread the remaining 4 slices of bread with 1 teaspoon of honey and place on top of the other slices.

Makes 4 sandwiches

SALSAS, SAUCES, AND DRESSINGS

- Hot Mustard and Sesame Dressing
- Thai Dressing with Fish Sauce, Fresh Chilies, and Lime
- Orange-Ginger Dipping Sauce
- Indonesian Peanut Sauce
- Anchovy-Lemon Butter
- Basil Aïoli
- Chipotle Mayonnaise
- Wasabi Mayonnaise
- Curry Mayonnaise
- Arugula Pesto
- Olivada
- Sun-dried Tomato and Black Olive Pesto
- Raw Puttanesca Sauce
- Tomato-Feta Sauce
- Jalapeño-Tomato Salsa
- Gingery Tomato Relish
- Carrot-Fennel Slaw
- Cucumber-Watermelon Salsa
- Jamaican Papaya and Avocado Relish
- Peach Chutney
- Red Chili Pepper Sauce with Raisins
- Cilantro Mojo
- Coconut Chutney
- Skordalia
- Spinach and Ricotta Pesto

 Was there ever a time, long ago, when people were happy to eat plain broiled chicken, pasta without sauce, burgers without ketchup? I doubt it. If you're like most people, the universal urge to easily dress up plain food has manifested itself in a motley collection of mustard, soy sauce, Worcestershire, and ragù housed on the door shelf of your refrigerator. You can do better, and the following recipes will show you how.

This chapter offers many opportunities for a quick flavor fix. These raw preparations can expand the possibilities of everyday cooking almost infinitely. A simple Arugula Pesto made in the blender in five minutes can be tossed with pasta or boiled rice, used as a condiment for chicken or fish, or even spread on crackers and topped with a sliver of sun-dried tomato. Indonesian Peanut Sauce can enhance the flavor of tofu, be used as a dip for raw vegetables, or tossed with cucumbers, scallions, and noodles for a simple main course. Chipotle Mayonnaise is a wonderful accompaniment to shellfish and seafood, and it makes the best BLT I've ever had.

Even though there are only two dozen recipes here, there are probably two hundred ways to use them. Some of these sauces will keep for days or even weeks on that same shelf with the A-1. If you can cook pasta, toast bread, buy a cooked chicken, or defrost frozen shrimp, you have eight months' worth of dinners on the following pages. ❖

Hot Mustard and Sesame Dressing

*I*n this dressing, smooth tahini (which is like peanut butter, but made from sesame seeds) is spiked with hot powdered mustard. The dressing is great on main-course salads of crunchy greens and chicken or seafood. I also use the dressing alongside rare grilled tuna and as a dip for steamed or raw vegetables. A colorful combination of snow peas, carrots, and red bell peppers is my favorite. (Tahini is available in health food stores and most supermarkets.)

2 tablespoons dry mustard

¼ cup tahini

2 tablespoons white vinegar

1 tablespoon honey

1 tablespoon soy sauce

¼ teaspoon salt, or to taste

2 tablespoons water (if using as salad dressing)

1. Combine the mustard, tahini, vinegar, honey, and soy sauce in a small bowl and stir until smooth. Let stand for 10 minutes to let the flavor of the mustard develop. Stir in the salt.

2. Stir in the water to thin the dressing if using it over greens. Stored in an airtight container, the dressing will keep in the refrigerator for 1 week. Bring it to room temperature (it will thicken in the refrigerator) before using.

Makes ½ cup; enough to dress
4 main-course salads

Thai Dressing with Fish Sauce, Fresh Chilies, and Lime

This is an incredibly versatile dressing—great on green salads or as a dipping sauce for seafood, beef, and pork brochettes. I like to drizzle this dressing over poached, sliced chicken breast and romaine lettuce or on top of grilled vegetables. Sometimes I use it to make coleslaw, mixing it in a big bowl with some shredded raw cabbage and carrots. Asian fish sauce, a staple of Thai cooking, gives this dressing its unique flavor. It's a nice break from the usual soy sauce and is available in Asian markets and most supermarkets. I've substituted maple syrup (only the real stuff—no imitation, please) for the more authentic but difficult-to-find palm sugar. If you can't find Thai chilies (the small, red, fiery ones) substitute a jalapeño or even some hot red pepper flakes.

½ cup lime juice

3 tablespoons Asian fish sauce

3 tablespoons maple syrup

1 small red Thai chili pepper or jalapeño pepper, seeded and diced, or ¼ teaspoon hot red pepper flakes

1 large clove garlic, finely chopped

Whisk together all the ingredients in a small bowl. Let the dressing stand for 15 minutes to allow the flavors to develop before serving. The dressing can be made up to 6 hours before serving and stored at room temperature.

Makes about ¾ cup;
enough to dress 4 main-course salads

Orange-Ginger Dipping Sauce

*T*his sauce gives life to plain poached chicken and steamed vegetables. It can also be tossed with noodles—Japanese rice noodles are quick and different (see Japanese Rice Noodles, page 56). Add two tablespoons more of peanut oil and it becomes a bracing salad dressing.

¼ cup peanut oil

4 teaspoons soy sauce

¼ cup orange juice

Grated zest of 1 orange (about 1 tablespoon)

1 clove garlic, peeled

One 1-inch piece peeled fresh ginger

1 jalapeño pepper, seeded and cut into several pieces

Place all the ingredients in the work bowl of a food processor. Process until the sauce is smooth and emulsified, scraping down the sides of the bowl once or twice as necessary. The sauce can be made up to 6 hours before serving and stored in the refrigerator.

Makes ½ cup; enough for 4 main-course
servings of chicken or vegetables
or 4 servings of noodles

Indonesian Peanut Sauce

*M*ade with items you're sure to have in your pantry even when the refrigerator is empty, this rich but simple sauce is great on grilled chicken and vegetables. Or instead of calling for takeout, toss it with noodles, chopped scallions, and cucumbers for a quick dinner.

½ cup smooth peanut butter

1 tablespoon Asian sesame oil

2 tablespoons soy sauce

2 tablespoons lemon juice

¼ cup water

1 small clove garlic, peeled

½ teaspoon hot red pepper flakes, or to taste

1 teaspoon sugar

Combine all the ingredients in the work bowl of a food processor. Process until smooth. The sauce can be made up to 3 days before serving and stored in the refrigerator.

Makes ¾ cup; enough for 1 pound of noodles or 4 main-course servings of chicken and/or vegetables

Anchovy-Lemon Butter

*F*ew recipes are so simple and satisfying. A pat of seasoned butter melting on top of a perfectly broiled steak or a piece of poached salmon is luxurious and even a little bit decadent. Anchovy-Lemon Butter is equally delicious on roasted chicken or baked potatoes. Any leftover butter can be tossed with hot pasta for a quick meal.

6 tablespoons unsalted butter, softened to room temperature

6 anchovy fillets, drained and finely chopped

1 small shallot, finely chopped

1 tablespoon finely chopped fresh parsley leaves

1 teaspoon grated lemon zest

1 teaspoon lemon juice

1. Combine all the ingredients in a small bowl. Mash with the back of a spoon until they are well combined.

2. Wrap the seasoned butter in plastic wrap and roll it into a 1-inch-thick log. Refrigerate until firm, about 1 hour.

3. When ready to serve, slice the butter log into thin rounds. The Anchovy-Lemon Butter can be stored in the freezer for up to 1 week.

Makes 6 tablespoons; enough to dress 4 steaks, 4 servings of chicken, or 1 pound of pasta

Basil Aïoli

*T*his is a classic garlic mayonnaise, with some basil added for freshness and color. I like aïoli with any fish or seafood—steamed clams and aïoli are a favorite in my house. It's also great with steamed vegetables or on top of baked potatoes. And, of course, you can use it as you would use plain mayonnaise. Mix a few tablespoons with some leftover chicken for a fantastic chicken salad, or spread it on a roll and top with grilled vegetables for a special sandwich.

4 cloves garlic, peeled

¼ cup tightly packed fresh basil leaves

1 large egg

2 tablespoons lemon juice

1 cup extra-virgin olive oil

½ teaspoon salt, or to taste

1. Place the garlic and basil in the work bowl of a food processor. Process until coarsely chopped, scraping down the sides of the bowl several times as necessary.

2. Add the egg and the lemon juice and pulse 2 or 3 times to break up the egg.

3. With the machine running, pour the oil through the feed tube in a thin stream. Process the mayonnaise about 1 minute, until thick and emulsified.

4. Scrape the aïoli into a small bowl and stir in the salt. Refrigerate until ready to use. Aïoli will keep in the refrigerator for up to 2 days.

Note: Raw eggs should not be used in food to be consumed by children, pregnant women, or anyone in poor health or with a compromised immune system.

Makes 1¼ cups; enough to accompany
6 main-course servings of fish or seafood

Chipotle Mayonnaise

*C*hipotle **mayonnaise**, made in the food processor in about three minutes, is fantastic on fried, grilled, or sautéed fish and seafood. The smoky Mexican chilies certainly wake up this classic dipping sauce. Chipotle mayonnaise is also great on all kinds of sandwiches—try it on a BLT and you'll see what I mean.

2 canned chipotle chilies in adobo

1 large egg

2 tablespoons lemon juice

¾ cup canola oil

¼ teaspoon salt, or to taste

1. Place the chilies in the work bowl of a food processor. Process until coarsely chopped, scraping down the sides of the bowl several times as necessary.

2. Add the egg and the lemon juice and pulse 2 or 3 times to break up.

3. With the machine running, pour the oil through the feed tube in a thin stream. Process the mayonnaise for about 1 minute, until thick and emulsified.

4. Scrape the chipotle mayonnaise into a small bowl and stir in the salt. Refrigerate until ready to use. The mayonnaise will keep in the refrigerator for up to 2 days.

Note: Raw eggs should not be used in food to be consumed by children, pregnant women, or anyone in poor health or with a compromised immune system.

Makes about 1 cup; enough to accompany 6 main-course servings of fish or seafood

Wasabi Mayonnaise

*T*he addition of wasabi (see page 7) to this mayonnaise makes it a perfect condiment for many Japanese-inspired dishes. If I want an elegant and unusual hors d'oeuvre, I spread this mayo on rice crackers and top with a little bit of chopped smoked salmon. Or I serve a spoonful of it on the side of rare-grilled fresh tuna. Sometimes I buy steamed, chilled lobsters and serve wasabi mayonnaise instead of melted butter. And there's always the sandwich route—rare roast beef and mayo on chewy bread never tasted so interesting.

3 tablespoons powdered wasabi

1 tablespoon lemon juice

1 large egg

1 teaspoon soy sauce

¾ cup canola oil

Salt to taste

1. Combine the wasabi and lemon juice in a small bowl.

2. Place the egg, wasabi mixture, and soy sauce in the work bowl of a food processor. Process until well combined.

3. With the machine running, pour the oil through the feed tube in a thin stream. Process the mayonnaise for about 1 minute, until thick and emulsified.

4. Scrape the wasabi mayonnaise into a small bowl and stir in salt. Refrigerate until ready to use. The mayonnaise will keep in the refrigerator for up to 2 days.

Note: Raw eggs should not be used in food to be consumed by children, pregnant women, or anyone in poor health or with a compromised immune system.

Makes 1 cup; enough for 6 main-course servings of fish, seafood, or steak

Curry Mayonnaise

A **little less rich** and elegant than homemade mayonnaise, this simple mixture (it's hardly a recipe) is still a treat. I use it with leftover steak or lamb to make tasty sandwiches. If you want to get fancier, use it on the side with sautéed soft-shell crabs or steamed mussels. And if you feel like throwing all restraint to the wind, slather it on a plump, juicy hot dog and toasted bun.

1 cup prepared mayonnaise
4 teaspoons curry powder
4 teaspoons lemon juice

Combine the mayonnaise, curry powder, and lemon juice in a small bowl. Refrigerate until ready to use. The mayonnaise will keep in the refrigerator for up to 2 days.

Note: Raw eggs should not be used in food to be consumed by children, pregnant women, or anyone in poor health or with a compromised immune system.

Makes about 1 cup; enough for 6 main-course servings of steak, lamb, or seafood

Arugula Pesto

This pesto, like regular basil pesto, has many uses. I've tossed it with pasta, of course, but also spread it on pizza (bake the shell and spread the pesto on right after it comes out of the oven). It's also great on a sandwich with a little bit of leftover chicken; and if you want to get really fancy, you can use it to make some Italian crostini—little toast rounds spread with a little pesto and topped with some chopped cooked shrimp (see Garlic Toasts, page 65).

2 small bunches arugula, washed and stems trimmed

2 tablespoons pine nuts or walnuts

1 clove garlic, peeled

⅓ cup extra-virgin olive oil

½ cup grated Parmesan cheese

½ teaspoon salt, or to taste

1. Place the arugula, nuts, and garlic in the work bowl of a food processor. Process until the ingredients form a rough paste, scraping down the sides of the bowl once or twice as necessary.

2. With the machine running, pour the oil through the feed tube in a thin stream.

3. Scrape the pesto into a small bowl. Stir in the cheese and salt. Pesto will keep in the refrigerator for 3 days.

Makes ⅔ cup; enough for 1 pound of pasta

Olivada

Olivada is a classic Italian black olive paste that can be used as a crudité dip, sandwich spread, or pasta sauce. If you use olivada over pasta, thin it by mixing it with two or three tablespoons of the cooking water before tossing it with the pasta.

1 shallot, peeled

1 tablespoon fresh thyme leaves

1 tablespoon drained capers

1½ cups kalamata or other large black olives (about 7 ounces), pitted

1 tablespoon lemon juice

3 tablespoons extra-virgin olive oil

1. Place the shallot and thyme in the work bowl of a food processor. Process until the ingredients are finely chopped, scraping down the sides of the bowl once or twice as necessary. Add the capers, olives, and lemon juice and process until a coarse paste is formed, scraping down the bowl as necessary.

2. With the machine running, pour the oil through the feed tube in a thin stream. Scrape the olive paste into an airtight container. Olivada will keep in the refrigerator for up to 1 week. Bring to room temperature before using.

Makes about 1 cup; enough for 1½ pounds of pasta

Sun-dried Tomato and Black Olive Pesto

I can never have enough sun-dried tomatoes, especially in the winter, when I can't get fresh tomatoes. The pungent, salty black olives make a fantastic contrast to the sweet tomatoes. I can think of many ways to use this sauce: spread on a sandwich of smoked mozzarella, as a pizza topping (just bake the pizza dough and when it comes out of the oven spread the pesto on it and sprinkle with grated Parmesan cheese), or as a condiment with grilled chicken. But my favorite is just to toss it with some dripping wet spaghetti and serve with a crisp green salad on the side.

15 sun-dried tomatoes packed in oil (about ⅔ cup), drained

8 kalamata or other large black olives, pitted

1 clove garlic, peeled

3 tablespoons whole fresh parsley leaves

¼ cup extra-virgin olive oil

½ teaspoon salt, or to taste

1. Place the sun-dried tomatoes, olives, garlic, and parsley in the work bowl of a food processor. Process, scraping down the sides of the bowl as necessary, until the ingredients are coarsely chopped.

2. With the machine running, pour the oil through the feed tube in a thin stream. Process until the ingredients form a slightly coarse paste.

3. Scrape the sun-dried tomato pesto into a small bowl. Add the salt. If the olives are salty, you may need very little salt. Pesto will keep in the refrigerator for up to 1 week.

Makes ⅔ cup; enough for 1 pound of pasta

Raw Puttanesca Sauce

*T*his is an even quicker variation on a quick Italian classic. It's perfect on pasta, of course. But if you don't feel like boiling water, it makes an unbeatable bruschetta topping. If you want to take yet another direction, try the sauce on top of grilled halibut or swordfish.

3 medium-size tomatoes, cored and cut into ¼-inch dice

¼ cup extra-virgin olive oil

4 anchovy fillets, drained and finely chopped

1 clove garlic, finely chopped

½ teaspoon hot red pepper flakes

12 kalamata or other large black olives, pitted and coarsely chopped

2 tablespoons drained capers

½ cup tightly packed fresh parsley leaves, coarsely chopped

Combine all the ingredients in a large bowl. The sauce, covered in plastic, can be stored for 3 hours at room temperature before serving.

Makes 3½ cups; enough for 1 pound of pasta or to generously top 6 large pieces of country bread

Tomato-Feta Sauce

*T*omatoes tossed with feta, cucumber, onion, and oregano make a natural pasta or bruschetta topping. For something a little different, I cook up some couscous (one 12-ounce box), mix it with this sauce, and serve it with something simple like spicy grilled sausages (see Couscous, page 116).

3 medium-size tomatoes, cored and cut into ¼-inch dice

¼ pound feta cheese, crumbled

½ medium-size cucumber, peeled, cut in half lengthwise, seeded, and sliced into ¼-inch half-moons

2 tablespoons finely chopped red onion

1 tablespoon fresh whole oregano leaves

3 tablespoons extra-virgin olive oil

1 tablespoon lemon juice

½ teaspoon salt, or to taste

Combine all the ingredients in a medium-size bowl. The sauce, covered in plastic, can be stored for up to 3 hours in the refrigerator before serving.

Makes 4 cups; enough for 1 pound of pasta or one 12-ounce box of couscous; or to generously top 6 large pieces of country bread

COUSCOUS

Couscous is a semolina pasta that's already been cooked and just has to be rehydrated quickly with boiling water. Okay, preparing couscous requires turning on the stove, but I'd hardly call it cooking. To make four main-course servings of couscous, bring 2½ cups water, ½ teaspoon salt, and 1 tablespoon extra-virgin olive oil to boil in a small saucepan. Stir in the couscous, cover, and remove the pot from the heat. Let the couscous stand, covered, for 5 minutes. Uncover and fluff the couscous with a fork.

In general, couscous can be tossed with any kind of pasta sauce:

❖ Tomato-Feta Sauce (page 115)

❖ Gingery Tomato Relish (page 119)

❖ Anchovy-Lemon Butter (page 106)

❖ Raw Puttanesca Sauce (page 114)

❖ Cilantro Mojo (page 126)

Jalapeño-Tomato Salsa

Of course, you can serve salsa with chips—it's almost as easy as opening a jar. But I like this spicy stuff tossed with pasta (add two tablespoons of olive oil so that it will cling to the noodles), and I especially like it with fluffy scrambled eggs, maybe a little Cheddar or Monterey Jack tossed in, and whole wheat toast on the side (see Perfect Scrambled Eggs, page 118).

2 medium-size tomatoes, cored and cut into ¼-inch dice

1 jalapeño pepper, stemmed, seeded, and finely chopped

2 tablespoons lime juice

2 tablespoons finely chopped red onion

2 tablespoons finely chopped fresh cilantro leaves (or basil or oregano)

½ teaspoon salt, or to taste

2 tablespoons extra-virgin olive oil (if using sauce for pasta)

Combine all the ingredients in a medium-size bowl. Let sit, stirring occasionally, for 15 minutes to allow the flavors to develop. The salsa, covered in plastic, can be stored for up to 3 hours in the refrigerator before serving.

Makes about 2 cups; enough for ½ pound pasta or 8 scrambled eggs

PERFECT SCRAMBLED EGGS

Great scrambled eggs are easier to make than a great omelet. I whisk them for fluffiness and make sure not to overcook them so I don't wind up with rubber. Whisk 6 large eggs, ¼ cup milk, and ¼ teaspoon salt in a medium-size bowl until the eggs are just a little bit bubbly. Melt 1 tablespoon butter in a medium-size frying pan over high heat. When it is bubbling, add the eggs and turn the heat down to medium. Push the eggs around with a spatula, scraping up the cooked parts and allowing the liquid to flow to the bottom of the pan. Cook this way until the eggs are just set, no more than a minute or a minute and a half.

For a quick breakfast, lunch, or dinner, serve scrambled eggs with:

- ❖ Jalapeño-Tomato Salsa (page 117)
- ❖ Ricotta and Chive Spread (page 23)
- ❖ Cilantro Mojo (page 126)
- ❖ Red Chili Pepper Sauce with Raisins (page 125)
- ❖ Tomato-Feta Sauce (page 115)
- ❖ Skordalia (page 128)

Gingery Tomato Relish

My mouth waters just thinking about a juicy, rare hamburger on a tender brioche bun topped with this chunky, pungent sauce. Since I was a kid I've eaten my burgers plain. But this topping has won me over. It's also great spooned over slices of grilled, broiled, or sautéed flank steak. I urge the vegetarians among you to try it on pasta or bruschetta—thick slices of toasted country white bread brushed with a little olive oil (see Bruschetta, page 120).

1 large tomato, cored and coarsely chopped

1 tablespoon finely chopped fresh ginger

1 clove garlic, finely chopped

½ teaspoon salt, or to taste

1 tablespoon balsamic vinegar

1 tablespoon extra-virgin olive oil

Combine all the ingredients in a medium-size bowl. The relish, covered in plastic, can be stored for up to 3 hours in the refrigerator before serving.

Makes about ¾ cup; enough to top
4 large burgers, 1 pound of flank steak,
or 4 thick slices of bruschetta

BRUSCHETTA—
ITALIAN GRILLED BREAD

Carbohydrate fiend that I am, I often make a dinner out of grilled bread spread with ingredients from my pantry or garden. There's nothing more soul satisfying than a few slices of crisp country bread perfumed with a little olive oil and some chopped herbs, then covered with diced ripe tomatoes sprinkled with a little salt and pepper. Warning: if you have a gas grill outside that you can heat up on whim, you also might become addicted to this "dish" (charcoal takes a little more motivation). (In the winter, I use my wide-slot toaster that can handle extra-thick slices of bread.)

To make grilled bread, place ¾-inch-thick slices of country white bread on a medium-hot grill and toast, turning once, until both sides are golden brown. Remove the bread from the heat. Rub one side of each piece with a peeled large garlic clove and brush with a little olive oil.

Also try grilled bread with:

❖ Chunky Artichoke Heart Spread (page 24)

❖ Lemony White Bean Dip (page 26)

❖ Roasted Red Pepper and Walnut Dip (page 27)

❖ Spicy Marinated Bocconcini (page 22)

❖ Ricotta and Chive Spread (page 23)

❖ Arugula Pesto (page 111)

❖ Olivada (page 112)

❖ Raw Puttanesca Sauce (page 114)

❖ Tomato-Feta Sauce (page 115)

Carrot-Fennel Slaw

*T*his simple mixture of thinly sliced vegetables is one of my favorite roast or grilled chicken accompaniments. Drained of its juices with a slotted spoon, it's wonderful on top of a turkey sandwich. I like to offset the sweetness of carrot and fennel with a little hot red pepper, but you may like it nice and mild.

1 cup finely julienned fennel (about ½ bulb)

1 cup peeled and finely julienned carrot (about 3 small carrots)

¼ cup white vinegar

2 tablespoons olive oil

¼ teaspoon hot red pepper flakes (optional)

¼ teaspoon salt, or to taste

Combine all the ingredients in a medium-size bowl. Let the slaw stand for 10 minutes. If the vegetables release a lot of water, drain some off in a colander before serving. The slaw, covered in plastic, can be refrigerated for up to 6 hours before serving.

Makes 2 cups; enough for
4 side-dish servings

Cucumber-Watermelon Salsa

*T*his salsa is adapted from a favorite recipe by Chris Schlesinger and John Willoughby found in their book *Salsas, Sambals, Chutneys & Chowchows* (William Morrow, 1993). It's got great personality of its own, but it won't drown out the flavor of lobster or any other seafood or shellfish you might want to serve with it.

½ medium cucumber, washed to remove any wax, halved, and thinly sliced

½ cup diced seeded watermelon, in ½-inch pieces

2 tablespoons coarsely chopped red onion

½ medium carrot, peeled, cut in half crosswise, and cut into matchsticks

2 tablespoons white vinegar

½ teaspoon hot red pepper flakes

1 tablespoon chopped fresh mint leaves

½ teaspoon salt, or to taste

Combine all the ingredients in a medium bowl. The salsa, covered in plastic, can be refrigerated for up to 6 hours before serving.

Makes 1½ cups; enough for 4 main-course servings of seafood or shellfish

Jamaican Papaya and Avocado Relish

A cold beer in one hand, a salty chip mounded with this relish in the other—party food doesn't get more fun and tasty than this. Try dipping cooked shrimp in it, too. I also like papaya and avocado relish on a simply grilled pork tenderloin or butterflied leg of lamb.

1 small ripe avocado, peeled, pitted, and coarsely
  chopped

1 small ripe papaya, halved, seeds scraped out and
  discarded, peeled, and coarsely chopped

1 small red onion, coarsely chopped

1 small fresh red chili pepper, or jalapeño pepper,
  seeded and finely chopped

1 clove garlic, finely chopped

2 tablespoons lime juice

2 tablespoons finely chopped fresh cilantro leaves

½ teaspoon salt, or to taste

Combine all the ingredients in a medium-size bowl. The relish, covered in plastic, can be refrigerated for up to 3 hours before serving.

Makes about 3 cups; enough for
6 main-course servings of grilled lamb or pork

Peach Chutney

*T*his exotic combination of fruit, chilies, and spices tastes great on grilled lamb or pork and complements fish steaks like halibut or swordfish. I also like peach chutney on a sandwich packed with thick slices of Virginia ham.

2 ripe but firm peaches, peeled, halved, pitted, and cut into ⅛-inch dice

½ cup raisins

1 teaspoon hot red pepper flakes

½ teaspoon ground cumin

2 tablespoons sugar

2 tablespoons lemon juice

½ teaspoon salt, or to taste

Combine the peaches, raisins, red pepper flakes, cumin, sugar, and lemon juice in a small bowl. Refrigerate for 1 hour, stirring once or twice. Stir in the salt. The chutney, covered in plastic, can be refrigerated for up to 3 hours before serving. Let the chutney come to room temperature before serving.

Makes 1½ cups; enough for 4 main-course servings of grilled lamb, pork, or fish

Red Chili Pepper Sauce with Raisins

*T*his flavor-packed sauce is great on plain chicken, beef, or pork. Spread it on a flour tortilla with some leftovers and you have a fantastic Southwestern sandwich. If you like your breakfast (or lunch or dinner) spicy, try it over eggs. Dried New Mexico chilies can be found in the produce aisle of your supermarket or in the spice section of your gourmet store.

4 dried New Mexico chilies

1 clove garlic, coarsely chopped

¼ cup raisins

¼ teaspoon ground cumin

2 tablespoons plain yogurt

½ teaspoon salt, or to taste

1. Place the chilies in a small bowl. Cover with hot tap water and soak until soft, about 30 minutes. Remove them from the water, reserving ½ cup of the liquid. Stem and seed the chilies; then coarsely chop them.

2. Place the chilies, garlic, raisins, and cumin in the work bowl of a food processor. Process until a thick paste forms.

3. Add the soaking water to the paste and process until smooth.

4. Scrape the sauce into a small bowl. Stir in the yogurt and salt. The sauce, covered in plastic, can be refrigerated for up to 6 hours before serving.

Makes ⅔ cup; enough for 4 main-course servings of chicken, pork, or eggs

Cilantro Mojo

*T*his garlicky, emerald-green sauce is a favorite condiment in
Spain. It's good, simple party food, scooped onto chips instead of, or
along with, tomato salsa. It invigorates plain grilled chicken or fish and
can also be served with goat cheese. (I drizzle it on bread spread with cheese.)

4 large cloves garlic, peeled

*½ green bell pepper, cored, seeded, and cut into a few
pieces*

1 cup tightly packed fresh cilantro leaves

½ teaspoon salt, or to taste

3 tablespoons extra-virgin olive oil

1 tablespoon lemon juice

Place all the ingredients in the work bowl
of a food processor. Process until smooth,
scraping down the sides of the bowl once
or twice as necessary. The sauce, covered
in plastic, can be refrigerated for up to
6 hours before serving.

Makes about ½ cup; enough for
4 main-course servings of chicken or fish

Coconut Chutney

*T*his chutney is a nice combination of strong, unusual flavors and tastes great on swordfish or mahimahi. It also stands up well to pork tenderloin, pork chops, or spicy sausages—all easy to sauté or grill in under fifteen minutes.

¾ cup sweetened flaked coconut

2 cups tightly packed fresh cilantro leaves

1 jalapeño pepper, seeded and coarsely chopped

1 tablespoon coarsely chopped fresh ginger

1 tablespoon white wine vinegar

2 tablespoons vegetable oil

½ teaspoon salt, or to taste

Place all the ingredients in the work bowl of a food processor. Process until a rough paste forms, scraping down the sides of the bowl once or twice as necessary. The chutney, covered in plastic, can be refrigerated for up to 6 hours before serving.

Makes 1 cup; enough for
4 main-course servings of chicken or fish

Skordalia

Skordalia is rich and creamy, like a Greek tartar sauce. This Greek condiment traditionally accompanies fried or salted fish or hard-boiled eggs. I like it with sautéed scallops or squid and a simple green salad on the side.

½ cup bread crumbs

¼ cup water

2 cloves garlic, peeled

½ cup blanched almonds

¼ cup extra-virgin olive oil

1 tablespoon lemon juice

¼ teaspoon salt, or to taste

1. Combine the bread crumbs and water in a small bowl. Mix until the water is absorbed.

2. Place the garlic and almonds in the work bowl of a food processor. Process until the nuts are finely chopped.

3. Add the bread crumbs and pulse several times to combine.

4. With the machine running, add the olive oil in a thin stream. Add the lemon juice and pulse once or twice to combine.

5. Scrape the mixture into a small bowl and stir in salt. Scordalia, covered in plastic, can be stored for up to 6 hours at room temperature before serving.

Makes 1 cup; enough for 4 main-course servings of fish or seafood

Spinach and Ricotta Pesto

Here's an unusual way to prepare raw spinach, adapted from my husband's book, *The Complete Italian Vegetarian*. It's a puree with ricotta, Parmesan, and walnuts, great for saucing pasta, topping bruschetta, or dipping raw vegetables. If using for pasta, reserve ¼ cup of the cooking liquid to stir into the pesto to thin it before mixing it with the cooked pasta.

2 tablespoons walnuts
½ pound spinach, washed and stems trimmed
1 small clove garlic, coarsely chopped
2 tablespoons olive oil
½ cup ricotta cheese
¼ cup grated Parmesan
Salt and ground black pepper

1. Place the walnuts, spinach, and garlic in the work bowl of a food processor. Process until finely chopped, scraping down the sides of the bowl several times as necessary.

2. With the motor running, pour the olive oil through the feed tube and process until a smooth paste forms.

3. Scrape the mixture into a medium bowl and stir in the ricotta, Parmesan, and salt and pepper. The Spinach and Ricotta Pesto can be refrigerated for several hours before serving.

Makes about ¾ cup, enough to sauce
1 pound of pasta

SIMPLE FRUIT DESSERTS

- ❖ Chocolate and Strawberry "Sandwiches"
- ❖ Prune and Bittersweet Chocolate Bonbons
- ❖ Apricots Stuffed with Almond Paste
- ❖ Banana-Hazelnut Smoothies
- ❖ Tropical Fruit with Lime and Ginger
- ❖ Spiked Watermelon Cocktails
- ❖ Grapefruit Drizzled with Campari
- ❖ Blueberries and Strawberries in Sparkling Wine
- ❖ Strawberries, Red Wine, and Cream
- ❖ Blackberry Fool
- ❖ Fresh Figs, Walnuts, and Mascarpone
- ❖ Melon and Mango with Yogurt "Crème Fraîche"
- ❖ Peaches with Ginger Cream
- ❖ Pineapple with Lemon Cream
- ❖ Plums and Blueberries with Sour Cream and Brown Sugar
- ❖ Peaches with Ricotta-Walnut Filling
- ❖ Grapes and Roquefort
- ❖ Maple Figs and Pecans over Coffee Ice Cream
- ❖ Double Orange Sundaes
- ❖ Rum-Raisin Sundaes
- ❖ Chocolate-Cherry Sundaes

Before I wrote this book, I had trouble imagining a dessert that didn't begin with creaming together large quantities of butter and sugar and didn't end with cake pans or cookie sheets cooling on a wire rack. Then I developed my first recipe for this book: Strawberries, Red Wine, and Cream. I stopped on the way home from work to pick up some local strawberries, famed on the East End of Long Island for their sweetness and flavor. I soaked them in a little bit of leftover red wine, spooned them into a few glass bowls, and topped them with fresh whipped cream. I was amazed at the simple beauty of my creation.

The following fruit desserts don't have many ingredients. So it's important that each ingredient be of the highest quality and freshness. In the recipes in this chapter, baking can't mask fruit that is past its prime. Poaching can't infuse unripe fruit with flavor. Always buy the best fruit, the best liqueur, the best ice cream.

Now I am a complete convert to no-bake desserts. Of course, I'll make a birthday cake for the baby. But when I have friends over for a pasta dinner, at the end of the meal I'm more likely to serve them fresh figs and walnuts with sweetened mascarpone than an apple pie. The most lovely desserts can be made from fresh fruit and a few simple adornments. Pretty dessert bowls don't hurt, either. ❖

Chocolate and Strawberry "Sandwiches"

Good bread, ripe berries, and chocolate. The improvisational attitude of this dessert makes it fun to eat. These sandwiches are great on rich brioche, but good white bread works well, too. Sometimes I pop the sandwiches in a 300°F oven for three minutes to soften up the chocolate. You don't have to—after all, that would be cooking. But if you want to, nobody's going to tell.

Two 3-ounce bittersweet chocolate bars (such as Ghirardelli or Lindt), broken into bite-size pieces

8 medium-size strawberries, hulled and thinly sliced

8 slices brioche or good-quality white bread

Arrange the chocolate and then the strawberries on 4 slices of bread. Top the sandwiches with the rest of the bread. Cut each sandwich into quarters with a sharp serrated knife for easier eating.

Makes 4 sandwiches

Prune and Bittersweet Chocolate Bonbons

I eat prunes like candy, especially the extra-moist and flavorful ones imported from France. A sliver of chocolate and an almond inside each of these bonbons makes them extra nice.

12 large pitted prunes (with smaller prunes you might need less chocolate)

12 whole almonds

One 3-ounce bittersweet chocolate bar, broken into 12 pieces

Slice the prunes in half, leaving the stem end intact. Insert an almond and a piece of chocolate into each prune and pinch the halves together to seal. The stuffed prunes can be stored in an airtight container at room temperature for 3 days.

Makes 12 bonbons

Apricots Stuffed with Almond Paste

*T*hese fruit and nut morsels are a great no-cook alternative to cookies or candy. They're not too sweet and they make an elegant bite along with a glass of dessert wine.

⅓ cup blanched almonds

2 tablespoons confectioners' sugar

2 teaspoons water

12 dried apricots, sliced in half

1. Place the almonds and sugar in the work bowl of a food processor. Process until the nuts are very finely ground. Add the water and process until a smooth paste forms. Scrape the almond paste into a small bowl.

2. Spoon some almond paste onto the center of each apricot. Press the halves together so that a little bit of the paste squeezes out around the edges (you'll get an Oreo sandwich effect). The stuffed apricots can be stored in an airtight container at room temperature for 1 day.

Makes 12 stuffed apricots

Banana-Hazelnut Smoothies

*H*ere's a frozen dessert that's fresher, more sophisticated, and healthier than any store-bought ice cream.

4 medium bananas, peeled and sliced into ½-inch pieces

6 tablespoons light brown sugar

¼ cup hazelnuts

1 cup ice cubes

¼ cup milk

¼ cup dark rum or hazelnut liqueur

2 tablespoons chopped hazelnuts, for garnish (optional)

1. Place the sliced bananas in a sealed plastic bag and put them in the freezer for 1 hour.

2. Place the brown sugar and ¼ cup hazelnuts in a blender and grind together until fine.

3. Place the frozen bananas, ice cubes, milk, and rum in the blender with the sugar and nut mixture. Blend until smooth. Pour the smoothies into 4 goblets or tall glasses. Garnish with chopped nuts, if desired. Serve immediately.

Makes 4 servings

Tropical Fruit with Lime and Ginger

*E*veryone who tries it loves this combination of tropical fruits, lime, and rum jolted by fresh ginger. This dessert is a refreshing but far from dull way to end a hot and spicy meal.

2 ripe mangoes, peeled, pitted, and cut into ⅛-inch-
   thick slices (see How to Peel a Mango, page 85)

2 cups cubed fresh pineapple

2 teaspoons finely chopped fresh ginger

2 tablespoons lime juice

2 tablespoons light or dark rum

Combine the mango slices, pineapple, ginger, lime juice, and rum in a medium-size bowl. Arrange the dressed fruit on 4 dessert plates. Pour any leftover liquid over each plate. Serve immediately.

Makes 4 servings

Spiked Watermelon Cocktails

I've always thought that tropical drinks are more like desserts than
aperitifs. You can serve these watermelon ices as exotic cocktails, but I
think they're a great way to end a summer meal. Save time and aggravation
by buying seedless watermelon if you can. Prepare your ingredients ahead of time,
but it's best to wait until the last minute to throw everything into the blender—
otherwise, the drinks may separate. When you're ready for dessert, just blend
and enjoy.

4 cups diced and seeded watermelon

4 ounces vodka or tequila

¼ cup lime juice

½ cup sugar

2 cups ice cubes

4 lime slices (optional)

1. Place the watermelon, vodka, lime
juice, and sugar in a blender. Purée until
smooth.

2. Add the ice cubes and blend until the
mixture resembles crushed pink ice.

3. Pour the cocktails into 4 tall glasses.
Garnish with the lime slices, if desired.
Serve immediately.

Makes 4 servings

Grapefruit Drizzled with Campari

*I*like slightly bitter **Campari**, the Italian liqueur, sprinkled over grapefruit. Sugar and lime zest add to the sweet-tart taste of this juicy combination.

2 large grapefruits (white or pink), peeled and sectioned
Zest of 1 lime
3 tablespoons sugar, or to taste
¼ cup Campari

1. With a sharp paring knife, cut away the tough membrane from the outside of each grapefruit section.

2. Combine the grapefruit, zest, and sugar in a medium-size bowl. Let stand for 15 to 20 minutes, stirring occasionally, until the sugar dissolves.

3. Spoon the grapefruit mixture into 4 dessert bowls. Drizzle each bowl with 1 tablespoon Campari. Serve immediately.

Makes 4 servings

Blueberries and Strawberries in Sparkling Wine

A nifty combination of the down-home and the refined, berries in sparkling wine can follow anything from burgers to lobster. I serve glasses of sparkling wine before dinner, reserve a cup, cork the bottle, and use the rest for dessert. Any good-quality sparkling wine can be used here, but I especially like a slightly fruity California blanc de noirs.

2 cups blueberries, picked over and rinsed
2 cups hulled, rinsed, and quartered strawberries
2 tablespoons sugar, or to taste
1 cup chilled sparkling wine

1. Combine the berries and sugar in a medium-size bowl. Let it sit for 15 to 20 minutes, stirring occasionally, until the sugar dissolves.

2. Spoon the sweetened berries into 4 dessert bowls or goblets. Gently pour sparkling wine over each bowl. Serve immediately.

Makes 4 servings

Strawberries, Red Wine, and Cream

This is an adult twist on a childhood favorite, strawberries and cream. The wine gives the fruit an amazing ruby-red glow. If your berries aren't perfectly ripe, sprinkle them with sugar, let them sit for 10 minutes, and then stir in the wine. Macerating will soften them.

2 tablespoons sugar
¼ cup dry red wine
1 pint strawberries, hulled, rinsed, and halved
1 cup heavy cream

1. Combine the sugar and wine in a small bowl. Stir to dissolve the sugar. Add the berries and let them stand for 15 minutes, stirring 2 or 3 times.

2. Whip the cream in an electric mixer until it holds soft peaks.

3. Spoon the berries and wine into 4 dessert bowls. Top with whipped cream. Serve immediately.

Makes 4 servings

Blackberry Fool

resh blackberries are a favorite luxury of mine. In this recipe, a "sauce" is made by macerating the berries with a little sugar. Half of the sauce is mixed with whipped cream and part becomes the topping. Of course, strawberries, raspberries, or blueberries can be used here also.

1 pint fresh blackberries, picked over and rinsed

3 tablespoons confectioners' sugar, or to taste

⅔ cup heavy cream

½ teaspoon vanilla extract

1. Combine the blackberries and 2 tablespoons sugar in a medium-size bowl. Mix with a fork, gently squeezing about half of the berries to release some of their juice. Do not mash all of the berries; leave some intact. Let the berries sit for 20 minutes or so, stirring once or twice to make sure that the sugar dissolves.

2. Whip the cream with the vanilla and remaining tablespoon sugar in an electric mixer until the cream holds soft peaks. Fold in half of the blackberry mixture. Spoon the blackberry cream into 4 dessert bowls. Spoon the remaining blackberries over each bowl. Serve immediately.

Makes 4 servings

Fresh Figs, Walnuts, and Mascarpone

Mascarpone is the Italian version of cream cheese. Rich and creamy with just a little tang, it's a distant, much more luxurious cousin to our Philadelphia brand. Sweetened with a little sugar, it makes a perfect accompaniment to ripe, fresh figs. The walnut halves look pretty on the plate and add crunch to this meltingly delicious combination. Sometimes I dust each plate with a little unsweetened cocoa powder for extra flavor.

1 cup mascarpone

2 tablespoons confectioners' sugar

8 ripe figs, halved from stem down

20 walnut halves

1 teaspoon unsweetened cocoa powder (optional)

Whisk together the mascarpone and sugar in a small bowl. Place a mound of mascarpone in the center of each of 4 dessert plates. Arrange the figs around the mascarpone and scatter some walnuts along the rim of each plate. Sift some cocoa powder over each plate, if desired. Serve immediately.

Makes 4 servings

Melon and Mango with Yogurt "Crème Fraîche"

*T*angy yogurt mixed with a little sour cream is a handy low-fat alternative to crème fraîche. I serve this melon-mango combination in glass goblets—it's so pretty and delicious. Avoid nonfat sour cream unless you enjoy the taste of glue; the regular sour cream called for here adds only 22 calories per serving, so live a little.

1 cup plain low-fat yogurt

¼ cup sour cream

1 tablespoon sugar

½ teaspoon vanilla extract

2 cups cubed honeydew melon, in ½-inch pieces

2 cups cubed mango, in ½-inch pieces
(see How to Peel a Mango, page 85)

Combine the yogurt, sour cream, sugar, and vanilla in a small bowl. Divide the fruit among 4 serving bowls. Spoon the yogurt mixture over the fruit. Serve immediately.

Makes 4 servings

Peaches with Ginger Cream

Here's a great combination of spicy ginger, sugary peaches, and cream. Other fruits can substitute for peaches—I like blueberries, mangoes, or plums. Crystallized ginger can be found in the spice section of your supermarket.

1 cup heavy cream

2 tablespoons confectioners' sugar

4 ripe, firm peaches, peeled, pitted, and each cut into 8 wedges

4 teaspoons finely chopped crystallized ginger

1. Whip the cream and the sugar with an electric mixer until the cream holds soft peaks.

2. Divide the peaches among 4 dessert bowls. Top with the cream and sprinkle with the ginger. Serve immediately.

Makes 4 servings

Pineapple with Lemon Cream

*T*angy sour cream and tart lemon complement the sweetness of fresh pineapple in this dessert. The lemon cream can also be used over any kind of ripe berries.

¾ cup heavy cream

2 tablespoons confectioners' sugar

3 tablespoons sour cream

2 teaspoons grated lemon zest

3 cups chunked peeled fresh pineapple, in ½-inch pieces

1. Whip the cream and sugar with an electric mixer until the cream holds soft peaks. Gently mix in the sour cream and lemon zest.

2. Divide the pineapple chunks among 4 dessert bowls. Top with the cream. Serve immediately.

Makes 4 servings

Plums and Blueberries with Sour Cream and Brown Sugar

I **absolutely love this** luscious way to show off perfectly ripe fresh fruit.

1 cup sour cream

¼ cup light brown sugar

½ pint blueberries

4 ripe dark plums, pitted and each cut into 8 wedges

Mound ¼ cup sour cream on each of 4 dessert plates. Sprinkle with the brown sugar. Scatter the berries and plums around the sour cream. Serve immediately.

Makes 4 servings

Peaches with Ricotta-Walnut Filling

*T*his recipe comes courtesy of my husband, Jack, whose specialty is Italian vegetarian cooking. It makes a great late summer dessert after a bowl of pasta with raw tomato sauce or a grilled pizza topped with olive paste.

⅓ cup shelled walnut halves

¾ cup ricotta cheese (about ½ pound)

4 teaspoons sugar

Pinch of nutmeg

4 ripe peaches, halved and pitted

1. Reserve 8 attractive walnut halves. Finely chop the remaining walnuts by hand or in a food processor.

2. Combine the chopped walnuts, ricotta, sugar, and nutmeg in a small bowl.

3. Spoon some of the cheese mixture into each peach half. Place a reserved walnut half on top. Place 2 peach halves on each of 4 dessert plates. Serve immediately.

Makes 4 servings

Grapes and Roquefort

*S*ome people consider cheese to be a forbidden food. Combined with seedless grapes, however, imported Roquefort (avoid bitter domestic supermarket blue cheese) is downright nutritious and a beautiful way to end a meal. This dish can also be served as an appetizer salad.

3 cups seedless red grapes (about 1 pound)

2 ounces imported Roquefort, crumbled

Combine the grapes and cheese in a medium-size bowl. Spoon the mixture into 4 dessert bowls. Serve immediately.

Makes 4 servings

Maple Figs and Pecans over Coffee Ice Cream

*T*his is one of the richest recipes I offer. The flavor and texture combinations of maple, figs, nuts, and coffee ice cream send me to heaven. If you have a decadent bone in your body, you'll love it, too. Any leftover sauce is great on French toast or pancakes.

½ cup dried Calmyrna figs

1 cup pure maple syrup

⅓ cup pecans, coarsely chopped

1 pint coffee ice cream

1. Place the figs in a small bowl and cover with very hot tap water. Let the figs sit in the water until softened, about 30 minutes. Drain them, remove the tough stems, and coarsely chop.

2. Combine the figs, maple syrup, and nuts in a small bowl.

3. Scoop the ice cream into 4 dessert bowls and top with the sauce. Serve immediately.

Makes 4 servings

Double Orange Sundaes

This is better than a Creamsicle. If you can't find blood oranges, use navel oranges—the color will be less dramatic, but the taste will be just as good.

4 blood oranges, peeled and sectioned

¼ cup Grand Marnier or other orange-flavored liqueur

2 tablespoons sugar

1 pint vanilla ice cream

1. Remove the tough outer membrane from each orange section with a sharp paring knife.

2. Combine the oranges, liqueur, and sugar in a medium-size bowl. Let the mixture stand for 1 hour.

3. Scoop the ice cream into 4 dessert bowls. Spoon the orange mixture over the ice cream. Serve immediately.

Makes 4 servings

Rum-Raisin Sundaes

*T*hese sundaes are more adult than the marshmallow and whipped cream variety, but just as much fun.

¼ cup dark rum
½ cup dark raisins
1 pint vanilla ice cream
2 tablespoons finely chopped almonds

1. Combine the rum and raisins in a small bowl. Marinate the raisins until the rum is almost entirely absorbed, 1 to 2 hours.

2. Divide the ice cream among 4 dessert bowls. Spoon the rum-soaked raisins on top of each, then sprinkle with the nuts. Serve immediately.

Makes 4 servings

Chocolate-Cherry Sundaes

*T*here's nothing better than sweet, ripe cherries—except for sweet, ripe cherries soaked in kirsch and poured on top of chocolate sorbet. It's 100 percent fat free, too. Look for chocolate sorbet in your supermarket ice cream case.

½ pound fresh cherries, pitted and halved

2 tablespoons kirsch

2 tablespoons sugar

1 pint chocolate sorbet

1. Combine the cherries, kirsch, and sugar in a small bowl. Let stand 30 minutes, stirring once or twice, until the sugar dissolves and the cherries soften slightly.

2. Divide the sorbet among 4 dessert bowls. Top with the cherries. Serve immediately.

Makes 4 servings

MENUS FOR A COOL KITCHEN

Here are just a few suggestions on how to use the recipes in this book. Take a look and you'll see how quickly great meals can be put together using one or several *Cool Kitchen* recipes. Choose from the following menus or just look them over for inspiration. Think about some of the eating you do—chicken, burgers, a piece of fruit—and see what a no-cook recipe or two can do to enliven your own everyday food.

Some of the menus that follow are entirely no-cook. Others require a modest effort—broiling (or buying a broiled) chicken or boiling some pasta. But all are flavorful, simple, and sure to delight family and friends.

Recipes with an asterisk (❖) are included in *Cool Kitchen*.

COOL KITCHEN COCKTAIL PARTY

Five-Spice Nuts❖ (page 13)
Marinated Black Olives with Orange and Fennel❖ (page 16)
Marinated Green Olives with Lemon and Thyme❖ (page 15)
Vodka-Spiked Cherry Tomatoes with Cumin-Cilantro Dipping Salt❖ (page 17)
Chips with Avocado Dip with Chipotles and Lime❖ (page 25)
Garlic toasts with Ricotta and Chive Spread❖ (page 23)
Cooked chilled shrimp with Wasabi Mayonnaise❖ (page 109)
Crudités with Roasted Red Pepper and Walnut Dip❖ (page 27)

PACKABLE PICNIC

Raisin and Honey-Roasted Peanut Party Mix❖ (page 14)
Carrot and celery sticks with Chunky Artichoke Heart Spread❖ (page 24)
Ham, Monterey Jack, and Chopped Hot Pepper Sandwiches❖ (page 89)
Fresh cherries
Apricots Stuffed with Almond Paste❖ (page 136)

Index